BLESS YOU,
Brother Irvin

The caterpillar club story

by John A. Neal

More best wishes from the author

John A. Neal

July 2006

Published by

GENERAL STORE
PUBLISHING HOUSE

499 O'Brien Rd., Box 415, Renfrew, Ontario, Canada K7V 4A6
Telephone (613) 432-7697 or 1-800-465-6072
www.gsph.com

ISBN 1-894263-94-4

Printing by Custom Printers of Renfrew Ltd.
Printed and bound in Canada

Cover design, formatting by Custom Printers of Renfrew Ltd.
The poem, *The Gift of Life,* is by the author.

Library and Archives Canada Cataloguing in Publication Data

Neal, John A., 1923-
        Bless you, Brother Irvin / John A. Neal.

ISBN 1-894263-94-4

        1. Parachuting—Anecdotes. 2. Airplanes—Fires and
fire prevention—Anecdotes. 3. Survival after airplane accidents,
shipwrecks, etc.—Anecdotes. I. Title.

TL755.N42 2005   363.1'2481'0922   C2005-903281-2

The Order of Exit*

* *"Order of Exit" refers both to the order for each member of the crew to bail out, and the order for each story to be presented in this book. Basically, the stories were presented in the order they came, not in any kind of chronological order.*

The caterpillar club story

The following is the story of how and why the club was formed, sponsored by Irvin Aerospace Canada Limited of Belleville, Ontario. This company was responsible, through their many worldwide branches, for producing the parachutes that saved so many lives, and enshrining forever the names of those saved.

Thousands of airmen, and a few airwomen, number among the most highly treasured souvenirs of their service a tiny caterpillar badge. It is their passport to one of the most famous flying clubs in the world: The International Caterpillar Club, all of whose members have saved their lives by the use of a parachute.

One evening in the early 1920s, Mr. Leslie Irvin, inventor of the modern parachute system, sat talking over a drink at McCoy Field, Ohio (near the site of Wright-Patterson AFB), with two American pilots—the first two airmen ever to save their lives with parachutes of his design.

"You know, Leslie," remarked one of the pilots, "we ought to start a club for guys like us. As time goes by, more and more fliers all over the world will owe their lives to your chutes; it should be quite a thing in years to come . . ."

Today the walls of an office of the Irvin Industries factory at Letchworth, Hartfordshire, England, are lined with steel filing cabinets containing the records of tens of thousands of airmen of all nations who have escaped death by jumping with an IRVIN parachute.

Files of the American and Canadian members are kept at the Irvin Aerospace plant in Belleville, Ontario, Canada, and a count taken in 1977 showed a membership of 11,332 men and twelve women.

Each one had been given a gold Caterpillar Badge and membership to the International Caterpillar Club, honouring the pledge that Leslie Irvin gave those first two fliers who saved their lives with his parachutes so many years ago.

(The Caterpillar is symbolic of the silkworm, which lets itself descend gently to earth from heights by spinning a silk thread upon which to hang.)

The First World War had been ended only a few months when Leslie Leroy Irvin, a twenty-four-year-old film stunt man from California, demonstrated his first "free-drop" parachute. He had made the chute himself on a borrowed sewing machine; so impressed were the flying safety experts of the U.S. government that they immediately adopted it as standard equipment for their military aircraft. Five years later, the British Royal Air Force followed suit, and Leslie Irvin formed his British company, with headquarters at Letchworth.

Already, before the British factory swung into production, the first life-saving jumps were being made in America, and from all over the States applications started to come in for the little gold Caterpillars. By the end of 1925, the club's membership stood at twenty-eight and included Atlantic flier Charles A. Lindbergh, then a cadet in the American Air Corps Reserve. Lindberg, incidentally, saved his life by parachute four times before he made his great solo crossing of the Atlantic in 1927.

The first RAF man to qualify for membership was Pilot Officer C.J. Pentland, number thirty-one on the club's roll of membership. On June 17th, 1926, he was practising half-rolls in an AVRO over Heswell Golf Course when the aileron controls went wrong. He was thrown out head first as his aircraft spun at 500 feet. "It was a matter of seconds before I landed, hitting the ground rather hard, but otherwise unhurt," he wrote to Leslie Irvin. "I certainly owe my life to the prompt way in which the parachute opened."

That letter was the first of thousands that Leslie Irvin was to receive from "satisfied customers." Every year brought more fan mail and, with the adoption of his parachute by other governments, he extended his factories to eight other European countries and to Canada and Australia.

By 1938, Caterpillar Club Membership had risen to 4,000 and included fliers from China to Peru and nearly fifty countries in between. Among the famous personalities wearing the treasured badge were America's General Doolittle, who bailed out three times and once cabled Leslie Irvin: "Airplane failed. Chute worked"; Germany's ace flier, Ernst Udet; Britain's Lord Douglas Hamilton; and a score of test pilots including Alec Henshaw, Geoffrey de Havilland, and John Cunningham.

The first clergyman to qualify for membership was an RAF padre, Squadron Leader K.C.H. Warner, who leaped from a crippled aircraft over the Egyptian desert, while Britain also claimed the youngest member, sixteen-year-old Denis Nahum, an Oundle schoolboy.

Until the outbreak of the Second World War, Leslie Irvin and his clerical staff at Letchworth were able to cope quite comfortably with the steadily growing membership of this unique club. A few dozen names were received each month, and these were inscribed on a roll of honour on a wall of the largest room of the factory. But as the RAF and the *Luftwaffe* clashed in the great battles over Britain and the continent, the monthly few dozen increased to several hundreds; and by the end of the war it would have needed every wall in the factory to record all the names of those who were accepted into membership.

Shortage of gold—and reasons of economy—made it necessary to substitute the gold Caterpillar Badge with a gilt one, but no person who applied, and could substantiate his or her claim to own one, was ever disappointed.

Into the trays of the filing cabinets went the names of some of the greatest air aces of the war: "Cobber" Kain, Sir Douglas Bader, "Bluey" Truscott, "Pathfinder" Don Bennett, and hundreds of others.

With them, too, each in its own individual and carefully indexed folder, went stories of escape, some so amazing that to read them makes the adventures of James Bond seem like child's play. Some of the fliers were blown bodily out of their aircraft during combat; some floated safely to earth with their parachute canopy ripped by enemy bullets; some jumped at 30,000 feet; others at 200 feet—or less.

More than 13,000 RAF officers and airmen wrote from prisoner-of-war camps to apply for their badges after parachuting from crippled bombers and fighters over enemy territory. Two brothers in Bomber Command bailed out over Germany within twelve months of each other to qualify for membership; and one sergeant-pilot wrote on a POW postcard to thank Leslie Irvin for an easy letdown "on behalf of my future—as yet unknown—wife and children."

Among these thousands of RAF men, only one airwoman received the coveted Caterpillar badge during the war: Corporal F.H. Poser, who jumped from 600 feet while serving with a meteorological unit in the Middle East. Since then, several other women have become fully qualified members of the club.

Workers at Letchworth came to know RAF airmen whose lives they helped to save. Caterpillar Club Members were frequent visitors to the factory during the war, and repatriated prisoners made their way there to tell of their drops over enemy territory.

The biggest favourite among the workers was flight sergeant "Dickie" Richardson, who was blinded over Germany and whose voice became well known to listeners of the popular *Wilfred Pickles* BBC Radio Program. The factory decided to "adopt" Dickie while he was at the "Guinea Pig" Hospital at East Grinstead. The workers made collections for him, sent him a radio set, presents on his birthday, and other gifts of cigarettes and chocolate.

The official membership of the Caterpillar Club is only a fraction of the total number who are eligible. It does not include, for example, the thousands of Americans who parachuted safely in the Pacific War, nor, of course, the *Luftwaffe* airmen, most of whom carried an Irvin-designed parachute, made at a factory bought out by the Nazis in 1936. Officials at Letchworth often wondered what they would do if enemy fliers applied for the Caterpillar Badge—as they were perfectly entitled to do. Fortunately the question never arose.

Altogether it is estimated that at least 100,000 persons—as many as would fill Wembley Stadium or the Rose Bowl—have saved their lives by Irvin parachutes.

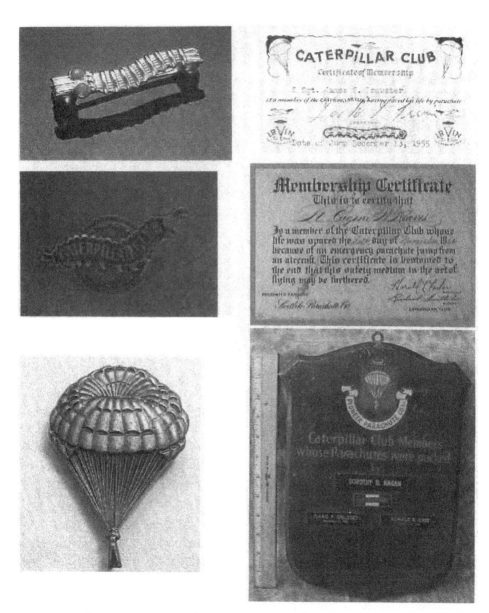

Pins, badges and membership cards for the Caterpillar Club.

Up to the time of his death on October 9th, 1966, Leslie Irvin was honorary secretary of the Caterpillar Club, and had been ever since its inception, but despite the fact that he had made more than 300 parachute jumps, he did not become eligible for membership—he never had to jump to save his life.

This brings up the reason for the author to have written a story on an otherwise innocuous creature such as the Caterpillar. As a member of the club, he has worn the badge on his lapel almost since the day he earned it over France. He is extremely proud of the symbol, and of course thankful that the parachute worked, but he is disappointed that so few people know what it means.

It is a very rare occasion when a passerby is aware of the Caterpillar Club, and its significance to the wearer of the badge. The author has been accused of collecting butterflies, or being a member of a club of entomologists; or some other meaning is ascribed to the pin unrelated to the saving of a life. The continual explanations of the meaning of the gold and ruby creature require more; it requires a book to describe the way it is earned, and why it is worn.

Initial studies indicated that very little has been published on this type of Caterpillar, outside of that issued by the clubs themselves. Local libraries possessed virtually nothing on the subject, save the story about Dolly Sheppard. The only way to get any real information is to ask the Caterpillars themselves.

In order to keep this book to a reasonable length, it has been necessary to limit the content to several dozen of the more interesting stories. The Caterpillar Clubs have many stories on file, and these files tend to swallow any storage space made available, no matter how large. Having it in a small book form will inform the reader without completely taking over his library.

Much publicity has been given to the few astronauts blasting off into space, with new worlds to discover. How about 100,000 aviators coming the other direction, with other discoveries to make? Like landing safely and walking away, for one . . .

I have provided a glossary at the end of this book to explain a few terms that may confuse the reader.

Bailout, Bailout!

These are by no means the favourite words ever to have been heard by an aviator! Unless they are uttered by a very sick mind, they mean that the airplane in which the aviator is flying at the time is in trouble. It is time to rejoin all the people on the ground. And the only way to do this immediately is to strap on the trusty parachute and jump out of the plane. The distance separating the plane from the ground is normally anywhere from about 500 to 25,000 feet (anything under 500 feet, forget it—you could hit the ground before the chute even opened; and anything over 25,000 feet you'll hardly remember).

If you are successful in getting the chute to open, then usually you will be treated to a nice, peaceful descent, provided the enemy fighters and the flak keep their distance—and it is the ground waiting for you, not the sea. But if you are not successful in having the chute open, then there are rumours that the chutes come with an ironclad guarantee; simply return home to base for a replacement.

But to be serious about a subject that is very serious in itself: all of the aviators who answered the order for bailout, and walked away from it after landing, became "Caterpillars." They qualified for membership in one of the Caterpillar Clubs around the world, and were eligible to wear the "Gold" caterpillar. A unique breed indeed!

"*Bombyx mori*"! Such an unusual, and prophetic, title for a very ancient creature. The silkworm, discovered many thousands of years ago, was responsible for saving many lives during the Second World War. Silk, one of the strongest of all fibres, was chosen to serve in the earliest parachutes.

The first actual known use of a parachute was in 1783 by French physicist Sebastien Lenormand. It had been well developed by the time of World War I, but was not often used during combat flying in that conflict. (However, see the story on Jordaki Kuparento, page 104.)

During World War II, all flyers on the Allied side, and many on the Axis side, carried parachutes. This device saved countless lives on both sides. By the time of this war, nylon had begun to replace silk as the main fabric of the parachute. However, shortly after the First Great War, Leslie Irvin of the Irvin Parachute Company, remembering the little creature who started it all, introduced the Caterpillar Club. The only eligible members were those persons who had, in order to save their lives, jumped from a plane, or other flying object, by parachute.

Ever afterwards, these members were entitled to wear the small gold Caterpillar with the ruby eyes as a symbol of their accomplishment, and to call themselves "Caterpillars."

The Irvin Company was not alone in the manufacture of parachutes or in the sponsoring of the Caterpillar Club. For many years, until the end of the Vietnam War, the Switlik Parachute Company was making the products necessary to bring these flyers safely to the ground. They were actually the first to build a tower designed to train airmen to use their products, and the first person to use it, on June 2, 1935, was Amelia Earhart, the famous aviatrix. Switlik claims to have some 10,000 escape stories in its archives in Trenton, New Jersey.

The following are the stories of a number of such Caterpillars, and what happened to them just before and after they found they had to "hit the silk." As earlier advised, the title of the story comes from the words written to Leslie Irvin by a young New Zealand airman after an Irvin parachute had saved his life, and ensured the existence of his future children.

Every one of us 100,000 or more Caterpillars have echoed that young New Zealander's words.

There are many other interesting stories besides those described here, and which need recording for history. The stories listed in this book are placed in order of receipt, not in any order by country of the flyers. If any person who has experienced an escape by parachute, or other who possesses the story of such an escape, wishes it so recorded, please contact the author through the publisher. Volume two is a distinct possibility.

one of the pioneer caterpillars

The "Bailout" of Dolly Shepherd in 1906

I t is quite possible that Dolly Shepherd and her friend Louie May, both parachutists, were among the very first "Caterpillars," some sixteen years before Leslie Irvin instituted the club. While many of the parameters utilized by more recent members of the club were not present, they did indeed save their lives by parachute.

Dolly Shepherd was a parachutist for Captain Auguste E. Gaudron, who produced aerial shows at fairs and other events around England. Miss Shepherd began parachuting in 1903 and spent the following eight years demonstrating her skills at this risky sport. As the airplane had not been fully developed during this period, all of her descents were made from gas or hot air balloons.

While the parachute, invented by Louis Sebastien Lenormand, had been used successfully during many drops from balloons, nobody as yet had invented the parachute pack or the harness. So, when Dolly and Louie "bailed out," their parachutes were already loose, although attached to the balloon by a cotter pin, to be pulled free at the start of descent; or by a piece of "cocoa string" that would break from the weight of the falling body. On using the first method, the parachutist would be suspended from the balloon during ascent; for the second, he or she would be sitting on the edge of the balloon basket.

The only "harness" used by the parachutist was a trapeze bar to hold onto, and a six-inch-wide strip of webbing between the legs to take the weight. An open canopy and a firm grip were the major safety factors of the early parachutists.

Sometime in 1906, Dolly Shepherd and Louie May agreed to do a double descent by parachute; that is, they would both drop at the same time from the same balloon, using separate parachutes. Both instruments were attached to the balloon by cotter pins, with pull cords designed to release the pins. The ascent went smoothly, and at about 3,000 feet, Dolly decided they should release and float earthward together, thrilling the many spectators.

But Louie's pin would not release! Despite frequent attempts by both women, Louie could not get her parachute free of the balloon. Meanwhile, they continued to rise, and at about 11,000 feet there was no sign of its beginning to start back down. Dolly, the more senior of the two parachutists, decided that the only way possible to save their lives was by using her parachute to bring the both of them to earth.

With Louie's legs wrapped firmly around Dolly's waist and with her arms around Dolly's neck, Dolly's cotter pin was pulled free. At first the canopy opened only partially, and the descent reached a fatal rate of speed. Then it fortunately opened fully and, while the descent was still far too rapid, the two parachutists did land safely. However, while Louie May was able to walk away from the drop zone, Dolly Shepherd was not, having been injured either from the fall or from the weight of Miss May. She spent months in treatment before she was able to return to her profession.

While there have been many parachute descents since that have possibly been as hazardous as that of Shepherd and May, I am not certain that I would have been able to hang onto a trapeze bar, or sit comfortably on nothing but a six-inch-wide webbing strip, during a descent—especially with an enemy night fighter continuing the attack, and shrapnel whizzing by my ear!

In addition to the thanks necessary for Leslie Irvin's work, we must also pass thanks along to whoever thought up the parachute pack and the harness. And, of course, to people like Miss Dolly Shepherd who went into this sport partly for the personal thrills, and partly to please the crowds.

But in the case of Caterpillars like myself, and most of those written up in other stories, crowds at the point of landing would have been a real problem!

This account is based on the story When the Chute Went Up, *by Dolly Shepherd with Peter Hearn and Molly Sedgwick.*

Dolly Shepherd.

sailing on the zuiderzee

The Bailout of Lt. Claude C. Murray on October 6th, 1944

"**I** had been hit and I didn't know where. A huge, huge impact and a big jolt shuddered through my body. Something had happened! Then my right engine burst into flames.

"Our training for various flying procedures had been so complete that the actions came automatically to me. Everything to the firewall! Drop the fuel belly tanks! But I had forgotten to switch from these to the main wing tanks. Without fuel, both engines started to windmill.

"Realizing what had happened, I switched to the main tanks and got the port engine going again, but not the starboard one, which was too damaged. By this time I was down to between 6,000 and 8,000 feet, but I could still fly on one engine! Then I decided it was time to go home.

"Smoke surged into the cockpit (smoke in an airplane can be very scary). 'Mayday! Mayday!' I called on the radio [the pilot's signal that means he's going down]. Below, I could see the vast expanse of the Zuiderzee. I had gone into Germany, flown back over Arnhem, and now was headed for England.

"I popped the canopy, and the suction took off my helmet, goggles, and oxygen mask. My helmet hadn't been buckled, but it didn't make any difference, since I couldn't talk to anybody on my radio. In the plane we had an IFF [Identification, Friend or Foe] system that was wired for safety. I broke the wire and pushed the switch, which created an automatic signal identifying me as a friend. If anyone was on that IFF channel, and I was in their vicinity, they would know that I was an Allied aircraft.

"The counter-rotating propellers came into play. When the right engine stopped, I kept a hard left rudder so the airplane would stay straight and level. I didn't trim it. What I was trained to do was trim the airplane, get into a slight climb, slow it down to 120 mph, slip out the side, and go down between the two tail booms underneath the horizontal stabilizer. These were the book's instructions, but a few pilots had been decapitated trying to follow them through!

"Still holding the rudder in, I stuck my elbow out over the side. The wind was so strong it almost tore my arm off. I was sitting on a seat-type dinghy with a backpack-type parachute strapped together below. I also had on the Mae West, which was strapped to the dinghy. How was I going to get out of this thing? 'I think you've had it,' I thought, and let go of everything. I took my foot off the rudder and prayed.

"The airplane, with the port engine propeller going counter-clockwise, flipped over, and I fell out. The next thing I knew, I was floating down in a parachute. We had been told to hang on to the D-ring for good luck.

"'Have I got the D-ring? Where's the D-ring?' I didn't know. Obviously I had pulled it, but didn't remember doing it. Maybe I had blacked out a little. I floated down in the parachute and didn't realize what had happened. I hadn't trimmed the airplane up so it could fly straight and level on one engine, and therefore it had simply flipped over due to torque.

"I was raised an Episcopalian. Even though I hadn't been to church in England, I knew what it meant to pray. I had a certain philosophy. Every time I got ready to take off on one of those four missions I told myself, 'Nothing's going to happen to me. I'm going to get out of this thing okay—fly this mission and come back flying.' I felt that confident. So, of course, I prayed to God that this would be the result. When I got hit, I had thought it just couldn't happen to me.

"I drifted down in the parachute. Below me was the damned water. Here's where my training would come in again. We were taught to loosen the chest buckle, and the two buckles on our legs, and slide out of the parachute just before hitting the water. This prevented our getting tangled up in the chute harness.

"At first I couldn't get one of the buckles undone. I was bobbing up and down in the water, and I finally got free of the parachute. I inflated the Mae West, which brought me back to the surface. It was connected, by a small strap, to the dinghy, which was floating on the water. Reaching down, I found the carbon dioxide cylinder in my uniform, inflated the dinghy, and scrambled in.

"When I got into the dinghy, I looked for the equipment that should be there: paddles, something to make a sail out of, a sea anchor, a bail-out bucket, a whistle, green sea dye. But there were only the sea anchor and the bail-out bucket to be found.

"The sea anchor is strung out in the back of the dinghy— something small on the front end and fanning into a funnel shape. With that trailing on a rope, it kept me going with the waves instead of against them. I didn't know how cold the water was when I hit it but now I was cold, cold, cold! There was a flap I could pull over myself but it didn't do much to keep the cold out. I just sat there in the dinghy and floated, wondering where I was, where I was going, and what was going to happen. I figured I would be captured.

"This all happened about 1300 hours, one o'clock in the afternoon. I couldn't see very much, although I guess I was only about a mile or so offshore. I didn't remember seeing the shoreline when I came down. And I was too worried about getting out of the parachute when I fell into the water. I sure didn't look around and say, 'Oh, there's Amsterdam over there and I'm splashing around in the Zuiderzee.' All I remember is that I got in the dinghy and floated there. The only warmth I was to have for the next thirteen hours came from taking a leak in the dinghy, and feeling that nice warm water down between my legs.

"Night came and darkness surrounded me. It must have been clear, because suddenly I saw on the horizon what appeared to be the low form of a boat, possibly what a submarine would look like. I started to paddle with my hands and I got to the shore. I had floated into a little island that turned out later to be the 'Fortress Pampus,' an old Dutch fortress about two and a half acres in size. It guarded the bay that I could see when I got up onto the fortress. I was about a mile from shore.

"I was tired after thirteen hours in a boat, and all I wanted to do was sleep. I crawled out of the dinghy and deflated it, then lay down underneath some bushes and fell asleep. When I awoke the following day, with my mind much more settled to my immediate future, I paddled my way across the Zuider Zee to the mainland, fortunately unseen, and started on my way towards freedom. Fortunately this was ensured when I was found by members of the Dutch Resistance instead of by members of the occupying forces."

From personal communications by Lt. Murray. He was flying an American twin-engined fighter, the P-38 Lightning. It possessed fuselages that were joined in the tail by a boom. This boom represented a decapitation hazard to pilots bailing out by the recommended procedure.

The Ditching Hatch Escape

The Bailout of F/O Donald H. Cheney, DFC, of the RCAF, on August 5th, 1944

"Lancaster V-Victor, Serial No. JB 139, KC-V, of RAF Bomber Command, with myself as pilot and captain, along with six other crewmembers, was operating with No. 617 Squadron. On August 5th, we were detailed with sixteen other squadron aircraft, all of us carrying 12,000-pound "Tallboys" bombs, to attack the U-boat pens at Brest in France. We were to arrive at the target in daylight, about 11:40 in the morning.

"Our plane was hit by flak during our bombing approach, with two crewmembers seriously wounded, and the aircraft on fire along the entire length of the starboard (right) wing. One engine had been knocked out. I gave the order to bail out just seconds before the bomb drop order was expected from the bomb-aimer. He released the bombs immediately, and they fell about 500 yards short of the target.

"The rear gunner and the mid-upper gunner bailed out by the rear door. The bomb-aimer released the nose escape hatch door, which then twisted across the opening, seriously restricting the room to escape. With the engineer, he then tended to the wounds of the navigator and wireless operator, and they helped the navigator to squeeze through the hatch opening. The engineer then helped the bomb-aimer to squeeze through, and then proceeded to the rear door for his own escape.

"I was left with the wounded wireless operator, whom I helped to the front hatch while still standing beside the pilot's seat. I was holding him with one hand, and the control column with the other. He was eventually able to squeeze through with my help. He could not have made it to the rear door with the heat building up in the cabin.

"Realizing that my only chance to escape now would be through the ditching escape hatch (over the pilot's seat), I pulled the release, which ejected the hatch cover immediately. I had been handed my parachute by one of the crewmembers, and had buckled it onto my chest hooks. I put the aircraft into as straight and level a flight as I could, and stood up on the pilot's seat. Then I started climbing out of the hatch.

"I could get my head out, but not the parachute pack on my chest. So I tilted the pack upwards and pushed it outside first, so my body would have room to exit. I stood on the armrests of the seat, and got my knees clear of the hatch. Then I put my left foot on the top of the armour-plated back of the seat, pushing out as far as I could. The airspeed increased as the plane began a shallow dive towards earth. I pushed straight up, and out, and was thrown free of the aircraft.

"The mid-upper gunner had fortunately lowered his guns, which I cleared by inches. I scraped my face on aerial wires, but fortunately did not get tangled in them. Twin fins whipped by, in my peripheral vision, and then I was tumbling free. Sky and sea and some land alternated in my view as I fell head over heels. I pulled the rip cord to open the parachute as soon as I was certain I was clear of the aircraft.

"But the wire release for the chute, and the handle itself, came away in my hand and I dropped them. (I thought, *Christ, the parachute is defective*!) Then a 'whump,' a terrific jolt, and I was hanging upright, from a huge canopy, at about 4,000 feet over a wide bay. The noise of the aircraft engines was droning faintly away in the distance, but the silence was otherwise disturbed only by the flap, flap, flap of the chute in the warm summer breeze.

"I had no sense of falling. It was more like being pinned to the sky and dangling. I could see whitecaps on the sea below. I looked around and watched my aircraft make several gyrations before diving nose first into the sea about three miles off a small island farther down the coast. I had feared it might crash into a small town on the island, and was relieved when this did not happen. With a burst of black smoke and dark orange flame, followed by a cloud of white steam and a hissing sound, the aircraft disappeared into the sea. Hundreds of small pieces splashed all around as it disintegrated.

"The silence was soon broken by the 'crackle' of a single Merlin engine as a clipped wings Spitfire V dove past me just fifty feet away. I could see the pilot's face clearly, as he had the canopy pushed back. Gave him the 'thumbs up' signal that I was okay. He returned my salute, made several passes and circles around me as I descended, then climbed off into the sky and disappeared.

"I realized the sea was suddenly getting closer, and very quickly, and then felt the sensation of falling, which was not really unpleasant. I hit the water, feet first, and somewhat sooner than I had expected. I went underwater slightly and took in a good mouthful of seawater. Then my Mae West opened and I started to rise back to the surface. The chute billowed out over the water behind me and settled on the water. The wind began pulling me across the water, so I hit the harness release and the harness fell away. The chute settled on the water. I realized I was very foot-heavy, as water had filled my flying boots and they were pulling my legs down and inhibiting my attempts to swim. I pried off my flying boots with my feet, and immediately became much lighter in the water.

"To my great joy, the water temperature was quite pleasant. I had been brought up near water and could swim well from an early age, so I was not unduly alarmed at being so far from shore. I emptied my pockets, including a couple of 'quid' and change

(English money), into the sea. I struck out for shore a couple of miles away, but I soon began to tire. Two hours later I was feeling cold, and could see shore fortifications and obstacles, so I turned back.

"As I did so, a fishing boat powered by an inboard motor approached, and I was quickly hauled over the side of the boat by the strong arms of six young French fishermen.

"A totally unexpected catch for them! But a welcome one for me."

From a personal communication by F/O Cheney

BLESS YOU, Brother Irvin

the wet noodle

The Bailout of Ralph K. Patton on January 5th, 1944

"Unfortunately for crew 38 of the 94th Bomb Group of the U.S. 8th Air Force, it was a beautiful day over Bordeaux, France, on January 5th, 1944. There was not a cloud in the sky as our B-17 led the high squadron off the target, the Merignac airfield, east of Bordeaux. German anti-aircraft fire was intense and deadly accurate; it blew a hole two feet in diameter in our right horizontal stabilizer, plus numerous smaller holes in the vertical stabilizer. This slowed our airspeed below that of the descending formation, and by the time we reached the south coast of the Brest Peninsula, we were about two miles behind the formation.

"As a straggler without fighter escort, in a cloudless sky, we were duck soup for the formation of German FW190s. They came up from Lorient as we crossed the southern coast of the Brest Peninsula at noon. As we manoeuvred to evade the third pass of the FW190s at 14,000 feet, the entire tail assembly of B-17 212 broke off, and the control column flopped back into my lap. When I pushed it forward there was no resistance whatsoever; it flopped back and forth like a wet noodle!

"By the time Glen Johnson, our first pilot, had sounded the alarm bell, I was out of my co-pilot's seat on the right side of the cockpit. Then I retrieved my chest pack parachute, which had been stored under my seat. While I struggled to attach my chute to my harness, the bombardier and navigator had jettisoned the lower escape hatch door, and had already left the nose of the aircraft.

"As soon as my chute was firmly attached to the harness, I dove head first out of the open escape hatch. The sudden rush of air, and my tumbling head over heels, completely disoriented me. I kept spinning for what seemed like an eternity—but actually was only a few seconds—until I experienced the sheer joy of discovering the D-ring in my right hand. Remembering my training, I thought that I should not pull the ring until I could see the ground. But the urgency of the immediate situation (probably complete panic, plus curiosity) compelled me to pull the damned thing, just to be sure it was going to work.

"The D-ring pulled easily and I could feel the rush of white nylon passing my nose. The monster white umbrella opened gently overhead and snapped my twisting, tumbling fall to a gentle, peaceful descent. Peaceful, that is, until the victorious FW190 seemed to be heading directly at me. Fortunately for me, the *Luftwaffe* pilot was not inclined to shoot, and peeled off at about 1,000 yards.

"I estimate that I opened my chute at about 11,000 feet, so the descent took what seemed like an inordinately long time. It was quite peaceful hanging up there, and I could hear dogs barking, and people talking (in a foreign language that I couldn't understand), and I had time to survey the countryside looking for a good spot in which to hide.

"About halfway down, I noticed that I was swinging like a pendulum, and I thought I ought to do something about that. Once again falling back on our one training class on parachuting, I pulled on the risers with my right hand. The harder I pulled, the more the right side of the chute collapsed. This scared the living daylights out of me, and I quickly decided that being a pendulum wasn't all that bad.

"As I neared the ground, I could see one of the famous Brittany 'hedgerows' coming up at me at what seemed like Mach II speed. As I descended, completely out of control, some guiding hand propelled me over the top of the 'hedgerow' and I collapsed in a heap at its base. I hit the ground on both heels; then my knees collapsed, and my backside hit the ground with a jolting thud. I was still in one piece and none the worse for the experience.

"I lived with a number of French families for sixty-two days, until I was returned to England via Reseau Shelburne's 'Operation Bonaparte' and MGB 503 on March 18th, 1944."

Ralph Patton was one of the founders, and is the current chairman, of the Air Forces Escape & Evasion Society of the U.S.A., formed to give evaders and escapers a means of thanking the people of the various resistance movements for what they had done for the members during the war. Very often, this help was extended only minutes after the flyer had become a Caterpillar. This story was taken from a personal communication.

The Caterpillar Club in postage—1985 and 1999.

The Big Sleep

The Bailout of F/O Tom Wingham, RAF, on April 22, 1944

Roger Freeman in his book *Experiences of War: The British Airman* devoted a bit of it to navigator Tom Wingham, in the chapter, "The Pay Off - The Wrong Side of the Drink." Tom at that time was on his second tour. He later flew on tour number three. But here's what Roger Freeman said, quoting Tom's words:

"God, its cold! Where the hell are the bed-clothes? What clot's pinched them? In reaching down to pull the clothes up my hand just grasped fresh air. The bed seemed much harder than usual and my pillow seemed to have gone as well, but at least the b..... had left me with the sheet I was lying on. Flat on my back I opened my eyes and gradually focused.

"Above me was the sky, dark but clear, with the stars just a blur. Damn! This was the first time I'd ended up in a ditch. However sloshed, I'd always managed to make it back to the billet before— but then, there always had to be a first time! Everything was so quiet. Not a sound to be heard, not a light in sight. What on earth was I doing in the middle of a field? And what were these cords doing tangled up with my arms? Groping around I gradually traced the cords which seemed to be attached to the sheet, but were also attached to the harness which was still strapped on.

"Then realization came. I was lying on a parachute. But how did I get here? How long it took while I gathered my senses together I'll never know. I tried to read my watch but, annoyingly, was unable to focus properly. Gradually, things became clearer. Dropping through the forward escape hatch, seeing the black bulk of the aircraft above me, pulling the rip cord, then—nothing, till I woke up on the ground.

"For a while I tried to reconstruct events to convince myself that we had completed our trip and I had bailed out over England on our return. But the true facts eventually came to mind. We hadn't reached the target and on our run-in to Dusseldorf the aircraft wing had caught fire somewhere west of Aachen and I was now on the wrong side of the Channel. Action now seemed to be imperative. I must hide the chute and run. But which way? I did not know on which side of the Dutch-German border I had landed, but south-west seemed the most sensible way to go.

"In one movement I hit the quick-release of the harness, gathered up the parachute, jumped up to run—and only to fall flat on my face. I was getting short on oxygen when I had bailed out and consequently was concerned about opening my parachute in case I blacked out. We had been at 19,000 feet. Failure then to follow procedure to protect my head had resulted in the heavy clips hitting me as the parachute snapped open, so knocking me out with—if one may pun—two perfect clips to the jaw.

"Being unconscious I must have landed like a sack of potatoes and my legs and back had been jarred. The knockout had produced concussion as a result of which my vision was blurred and this was to remain so for the next two or three weeks. However, I was alive and perhaps ignorance is bliss, for I was to find out later that I was the only member of the crew to come out without a scratch. Two were killed, one blown out of the aircraft to have a leg amputated; one with a torn thigh—but who was looked after and patched up by a sympathizer; one with a broken ankle; and the other with a sprain. It seemed in retrospect that I was lucky to be knocked out."

The foregoing is No. 76 Squadron navigator Tom Wingham's personal account, when he had the realization that his Halifax had been shot down and he was in a foreign land. A parachute descent in darkness was fraught with danger as, unable to see where they were going, many men were injured and some killed.

There were many stories about these dangers, including one heard years ago from a Caterpillar whose story is unfortunately not in this book: As he neared the ground, his parachute started to swing wildly. In the final few feet, the parachute swung him into the brick wall of a building, knocking him out. He came to three days later, many miles from the drop zone, with no memory of what had gone on during those three days!

out of italy

The Bailout of Lt. Harold E. Cook on May 24th, 1944

L t. Harold E. Cook was a navigator in a B-24 Liberator, flying with the 722nd Bomb Squadron, of the 450th Bomb Group, "The Cottontail Group," of the 15th U.S. Air Force, flying out of Manduria in Italy. The target of the day was Weiner Neustadt in Austria. The following is how Lt. Cook tells it:

"*The Attack* . . . As the formation turned at the initial point, about thirty-five miles southwest of the target, sixty German ME–109 and FW–190 fighters began making attack passes through the formation. Suddenly our plane was hit; there were loud metallic thumping noises, and the craft shuddered. My navigation table disintegrated behind me. I saw one fighter destroyed by our gunners, and it went spinning earthward.

"We were out of the formation now and additional enemy attacks were pressed, the plane sustaining heavy damage. Windows and gun turrets were shattered and one of our engines was set on fire. The first pilot was severely wounded and, unknown to me at the time, three of our gunners in the rear of the plane had been killed.

There was a stinging sensation in my back. Enemy machine-gun and 20mm cannon fire had done its job; we were helpless. The order to bail out was given.

"*The Bailout* . . . As I moved back towards the bomb bay to bail out, someone said, 'Drop the bombs!' (it was our Group's practice to have the navigator drop the bombs). Since the hydraulic system was destroyed, the only way to open the bomb bay doors, and permit crewmembers to bail out, was to smash the doors off by releasing the bombs. I dropped the bombs, and the bomb bay doors were gone. I crawled up to the flight deck and found the co-pilot still at the controls of the ship. I motioned to him to come and he nodded and started to get up. Suddenly the plane made a violent manoeuvre, and I was thrown out of the ship.

"I remember . . . I was falling through clouds above German-occupied Austria. I could see the ground, as I was fully conscious. Then at about 5,000 feet I pulled the rip cord; the parachute opened, and the force sent the air bellowing from my lungs. Then there was a wonderful silence; for now the sounds of air battle were far away. It was unreal being shot down; it is something that happens to someone else, never you. Only moments before, I had been part of a seasoned crew, and now I was headed to an uncertain future.

"*The Landing* . . . The ground was plainly visible now; I had descended through two cloud layers. The tingling in my back was a wound; the blood felt cool and wet. I was dropping down into a forest. The shock of landing stunned me momentarily. Luckily I came down in a small clearing and the chute dropped obediently behind me. I quickly unbuckled my chute and concealed it.

"I ran to the top of a ridge about 200 yards away and hid in the undergrowth. I could see armed civilians out looking for me. I dressed my wounds and surveyed my possessions; my escape kit included some German and British money and a candy bar. I also had a knife and a .45-calibre pistol. I was fully confident of walking out of Austria and reaching the Yugoslav partisans. When it was dark, I ventured down the small road and started walking southward. At one point, some civilians rounded the road and there was nowhere for me to hide. But it was very dark, so I walked towards them whistling. It worked, since they passed without a comment.

"I began to ponder what was ahead for me, alone, in an enemy country, and at least 150 miles from friendly partisans. After five hours of walking, I again crawled into some underbrush and quickly fell asleep. During the next two days, I chose to move south and east through forested and mountainous areas, where there was no food and often no water. Hunger was starting to weaken me. In three days I had travelled about thirty miles on less than 500 calories of food.

"*The Capture* . . . I spotted a remote farmhouse. Intelligence officers had indicated that if help was available in Austria, it would most likely be given by peasants. I approached a farmer and asked him for food. He provided milk and bread, but also a one-way ticket to a prisoner-of-war camp! Two armed civilians soon came through the gate to the farm and informed me that I was their prisoner."

From Lt. Cook's personal narration of his life after the attack. He was a POW from late May of 1944 until mid-April of 1945, when he escaped from the Big March. He reached Switzerland on April 24th.

get the Hell out!

The Bailout of Lt. E. Robert Kelley on September 5th, 1944

L t. Kelley was a pilot flying B–17s with 322nd Squadron, from 91st Bomb Group, of the 8th U.S. Air Force. His base was at Bassingbourne, just south of Cambridge, and normally a permanent RAF base. On September 5th, the crew's name came up for a mission on the I.G. Farberen Tool and Die Works at Ludwigshafen in Germany. Their plane lost two engines on the way to the target, and they were forced to turn back when the German fighters decided to attack their wounded aircraft.

"The German ME–109 fighters hit us from out of the clouds behind us, killing the tail gunner, destroying part of the rudder and elevator, and cutting off our communications with the rear of the plane. After a couple more hits on the wing near the #3 engine, we were down to about 6,000 feet and there was still no sign of an opening in the ground cover. I rang the bailout bell and told the navigator, bombardier, and engineer to go. I trimmed the aircraft, stowed down as best I could, and set the autopilot. Then I told co-pilot Lt. Anderson to go. He stood behind my seat and gave me a pep talk. 'Don't worry, everything is going to be OK. I'll see you on the ground . . .' I finally told him to get the h—- out. He disappeared into the crawl space to the door on the navigator's compartment where the others had gone to jump.

"Finally alone, I left the pilot's seat to put on my chute and was horrified to find that it wasn't hanging on the back of my seat. 'God!' I thought, 'I forgot my chute back in England!' A terrible feeling came over me until I looked at the co-pilot's seat, and saw Anderson's parachute hanging there. In the excitement and while giving me that pep talk, he had put on my chute! Relieved, I put on his chute, just as a big hit on the left wing shook the whole plane. I left 'My Baby' via the same door as the others. As soon as I jumped, I pulled the rip cord on my parachute. This was a big mistake, as I was still travelling at the aircraft's initial speed. With an altitude of 5,000 feet, I should have taken free fall for a while. Then I received my second shock of the day: the parachute didn't open!

"The spring popped in the pilot chute cover, so, in desperation, I tore at the pilot chute and threw it out. The shroud lines came out, singeing my hands, and the chute opened. I suspect I was tumbling, as there was a terrific jerk. Soon I was hanging from the open chute. I saw the B–17 going away somewhat above me, and I was shocked at the damage to the tail section just above the tail gunner position. Then, amazingly, I saw an ME–109 pass some 1,000 yards in front of me, chasing 'My Baby.' It was beautifully marked and I could plainly see the pilot leaning forward, and shooting at the B–17 as he closed in.

"I didn't watch him long, for I became aware of a second ME–109 coming out of the clouds. He spotted me, turned off his run at the bomber, and came towards me with his guns firing. He passed directly over the parachute. I looked up to see six holes in the fabric. I don't know whether he intended to set it afire, spill it, or hit it—or, more likely, just hit me. I recall pulling on the lines and shaking my fist at him, two rather stupid moves. I entered a second layer of clouds just as he passed over again, and didn't see anything else until I came out of the mist and the rain about 300 feet above the ground.

"I could see a farmer running a tractor in a field, and a colliery or a mine on one side of a valley. Then I noted that I was headed for the only woods around. In fact, I was drifting quite swiftly in the wind right to the centre of a four-square-block area of dense woods. I was also amazed to see that my B–17 had done a full 180-degree turn, and was now coming towards me, but half a mile or so away and headed for a small town. The woods were coming up so fast that I closed my eyes and doubled up my legs, which I had read somewhere was SOP (Standard Operating Procedure). The last thing I saw was the B–17 passing directly over the town (which I later learned was called Bazailles), missing the city hall and a church steeple by just a few feet, and crashing in a field just outside of town, with a tower of flame.

"I opened my eyes and found I was sitting, unhurt, in a hazelnut bush. My chute had hooked on a beech tree and swung me gently to the ground. I had no idea of where I was. It could have been Belgium, Luxembourg, France, or even (if we had drifted north) Germany. Soon I was given sanctuary by the Resistance forces and was an evader for the balance of my war."

Another story received by mail with permission to use. Robert Kelly is a member of the Air Forces Escape and Evasion Society in the USA.

The scheidhauer experience

The Several Escapes of Bernard Scheidhauer during World War II

This is the story of a brave young Frenchman who defied all the odds to help overcome the Nazi hordes who had enslaved his country during World War II. During his war, he made at least three escapes, only one of which would qualify him for the Caterpillar pin, but one of which caused his death.

At the start of the war, Bernard was living in Brest, which is the capital of the French province of Brittany. Although he was not one of the greatest of academics, he did excel at sports. All this time, his hopes and aspirations were to become a pilot following his graduation. This wish was unfortunately postponed by the fall of France in May of 1940, and pilot training would be denied to him as long as the Germans were in his country. So all summer long his plans were being made to escape France for England and to join the Royal Air Force.

Bernard, little more than a teenager, first tried to make a crossing of the Pyrenees mountains into Spain, but this attempt failed. He then decided, later in the summer, that he would try to escape by boat for the crossing over to England. But he could not do this by himself; he needed others to share the effort, the cost, and the risks, for the glory of serving France. There were brothers Jean and Guy Vourc'h, the latter a medical student, Marcel Laurent, Charles de la Patelliere and Robert Alaterre. A boat, the *Petite Anna*, was found at Douarnenez on the coast just south of Brest, and Guy Vourc'h completed the task of purchasing it for the crossing. As soon as he had assured the owner that it would be returned, the boat was his. Unfortunately he was unable to verify how or when the return would take place.

Scheidhauer and the owner tested the motor, although they did have to cut back on the time required, and this would cause them problems later in the voyage. The compass was set by a friend, Chancerelle, and the navigation plans by Marcel Laurent. Each of the crewmen had his tasks to perform, which would, hopefully, land them on the coast of Cornwall.

However, one old-time sailor commented that the *Petite Anna* was 99% more likely to be their coffin than their salvation; and the voyage very nearly confirmed this prediction. They started out on October 20th during a very dark evening, with another boat leading the way out of the bay. Soon the island of Tristan showed up, the lead boat turned back, and the *Petite Anna* went on to gain the open sea.

During preparations for what they hoped would be a fast crossing, the sailors had loaded only 180 litres of petrol, which they thought should last until they reached England. For provisions, they carried a few loaves of bread, some boxes of sardines, seven bottles of wine, three chocolate bars, a litre of rum, and enough water for twenty-four hours. They planned to be in Falmouth or Penzance around nine o'clock the following morning.

In order to avoid any German patrols, they skirted far to the west of the Island of Ouessant, off the Brittany coast, thus using up both time and fuel. By six o'clock in the morning, the engine, low on fuel, quit, with the English coast still not yet in sight, and nothing but the calm sea for as far as the eye could see. Unfortunately, Guy Vourc'h now took the occasion to get quite seasick, and was prostrate for the following four days.

About ten o'clock on the second evening, a violent wind came up from the northeast, which was the direction they were trying to travel. They used up what little fuel they had left bucking this wind. The boat, while having a mast, was not designed to use sail for anything major. All night long, the boat was tossed around like a cork, one moment up on the crest of a wave, and moments later, hurled down fiercely into the sea. They all kept their eyes peeled but could see nothing on the horizon. The storm kept up from the 22nd to the 26th of October, with no respite. They were about out of food and water, and forced into discussions of making some kind of soup using the leftover sardine oil with seawater.

On October 25th, three German planes passed over without spotting them, and continued on to the northwest. On the 26th, two more flew past at sea level, but fortunately did not fire at them. Jean Vourc'h wanted to hang up his white shirt on the mast as a sign of distress; he thought life as a prisoner might be preferable to drowning at sea. One advantage they had was that it seldom rained when the wind was from the northeast, so they had no problems from this except for the lack of drinking water.

By October 27th, they had the impression that the wind was calming. It became far less strong and changed directions to the southeast. Again, this was not the best direction, as it would take them slowly back towards the coast of Brittany. However, the sail did act as a rudder to keep them on the way to England. The passengers were by now worn out, dehydrated, and becoming the victims of hallucinations. The dreams of drinking water became an obsession. But on October 30th, the wind changed again towards the northeast, this time in a favourable direction. But the sea still had the same swells and the sky was still gray and low. At about three o'clock in the afternoon, the winds picked up again, and by five it was raining. Not a heavy rain, but more of a light sprinkle. Still they were able to gather some soft drinking water, which tasted just great after nothing but seawater for several days.

Through the whole night, the wind and the swells and the spray continued until the following morning, when they spotted some small islands just off the coast of Pembrokeshire in Wales. About eleven o'clock, they saw an enormous rock, desolate and with no signs of life. The *Petite Anna* passed it close to a huge reef where the foaming surf threatened the very stability of their boat. By this time, all of the other passengers were joining Guy Vourc'h in offering prayers for their deliverance.

Finally their prayers were answered; an English merchant ship, the S.S. *Craighorn*, hove into view. Intrigued by the presence of a small boat in these inhospitable waters, and obviously in difficulty, the ship stopped and picked up the desperate Frenchmen. They were fed and given what they needed to recover their composure. By nightfall on October 31st, the *Craighorn* entered the port of Milford Haven with six very relieved passengers on board.

After being cleared by the curious British, on November 5th, 1940, Bernard enlisted in the Free French Navy, serving on a ship called *Volontaire*, which was berthed in Liverpool. However, his ambition to be a pilot was answered on January 22nd, 1941, when he was called to Camberley to start his training. After Elementary Flying Training Schools (EFTS) and Operational Training Units (OTU), around June 24th of 1942 he received his wings, and was posted to join 242 Squadron of the RAF, who were flying Mk V Spitfires. The squadron was predominately staffed by Canadian pilots, and Douglas Bader, by this time nine months a prisoner of war, had once been the commanding officer of the unit . . .

Bernard flew on several sorties with 242, including sweeps over Dieppe during the ill-fated raid on August 19th, but no combat records are on file. On September 1st, 1942, P/O Scheidhauer, along with P/O Henri de Bordas and P/O Stourm, were transferred to 131 (County of Kent) Squadron, a fighter unit equipped with Presentation Spitfires paid for by the people of Kent. Bernard was soon in action, taking part in several fighter sweeps and scrambles. He was reported to sneak off from England in his Spitfire and fly low over his parents' apartment in Brest by way of saying hello, and then take a pot shot or two at ground targets of opportunity before hustling back to England.

On Remembrance Day, November 11th, Bernard's squadron was assigned to test out some new flight tactics about fifteen miles off the French coast. Part of the squadron orbited at 16,000 feet, serving as decoys while the balance did the same at sea level.

When the *Luftwaffe* did not fall for the "new tactic," the squadron set off for home at about 4,000 feet.

Flying in sections in line astern, the Yellow and Blue sections ran into a huge, towering cumulus cloud about twenty-five miles off Shoreham in England. Yellow Section was able to swing away and miss most of the cloud, but the following Blue Section, of which Bernard was a member, flew straight into the densest part. The planes were only about ten to fifteen yards apart. Right away they lost visibility and the air became so bumpy as to make flying very difficult. In a couple of minutes, Bernard saw another plane right in front of him. Trying his left control stick and rudder, he started a diving turn away, but his propeller caught the plane ahead, removing about eighteen inches from Bernard's propeller blades. Because of the bumpy conditions, Bernard did not quite realize at first what he had done, nor of the fatal nature of the collision.

Continuing his dive, Bernard came out of the cloud at about 2,000 feet. Then his engine froze, and, without any power, it became time to make use of his parachute. Turning onto his back, he dropped out of the cockpit, quickly pulled the rip cord, and within minutes of floating down was in his dinghy in the English Channel. The other Spitfires had followed him down to circle him, and he waved at them. Of course they could only relay his position back to England so others could come and make the rescue.

Pilot Officer "Taffy" Williams, who had been the pilot of the other Spitfire, was unfortunately unable to bail out and went into a gentle dive after the collision, to finally crash into the sea. He did not survive the crash, but his body was recovered by a Walrus from Air-Sea Rescue Squadron 277, based at Shoreham. Both pilots were about twenty-two miles off the English coast.

The same Squadron sent out another Walrus, piloted by Flying Officer M.F. Dekyvere and crewed by Sgts. E. Quick and Dizzy Seales, who found Bernard and took him safely aboard. The search took well over an hour before they spotted the dinghy and were able to land on the sea.

As a result of his later incarceration in the infamous *Stalag Luft* III at Sagan, and his participation in "The Great Escape," Bernard was never able to enjoy his new membership in the Caterpillar Club, or wear the treasured Caterpillar pin.

After he was taken back to England from his ordeal, Bernard was sent on a week's recovery leave in order to get over the collision with his squadron mate. Then, sadly, on his next patrol to the French coast, November 18th, Bernard was hit by flak that cut his fuel lines. Then, thinking he was heading for home, he for some reason headed *west* instead of *east*. He finally ran out of fuel and was forced to crash land, with his wheels up, by the Dielament Manor, near Victoria Village on the Island of Jersey, just barely missing a herd of cows. The island was occupied by units of the German Army.

At first, thinking he was on the Isle of Wight, Bernard wanted to return to base. Then when he was told where he was by the bystanders, he wanted to destroy his plane, but without a lot of success. These bystanders helped him to dismantle some parts of it, including the cockpit and the laminated wooden propeller, before the German occupying forces showed up about forty-five minutes later.

Bernard was taken prisoner and, after the usual formalities, he was assigned to the Sagan Prisoner of War Camp—*Stalag Luft* III. The almost undamaged Spitfire was turned over to the *Luftwaffe*, who repainted it in their colours and replaced the Rolls-Royce Merlin engine with a Daimler-Benz engine. Fortunately, the modified Spitfire did not perform nearly as well as its predecessor, or General Adolph Galland of the *Luftwaffe* might have had part of his wish, when asked by Hitler what he needed most to defeat the Royal Air Force *(his answer was, "A Squadron of Spitfires")*.

Being trilingual in French, English and German, Bernard's talents were soon picked up by the camp escape committee, which was headed by "Big X," Squadron Leader Roger Bushell. Roger was quite experienced in escape, and soon selected Scheidhauer to form a part of the security side of the escape and tunnelling operations. Bernard's first main task was to keep a watch on the German guards and report on their every move. When the tunnelling started, he also spent several hours at the tunnel face— a particularly hazardous task, with the constant risk of cave-ins and of being buried alive under all that sandy yellow soil. Fortunately, an ingenious method for the removal of that soil had been devised by another prisoner, Lt Peter ("Hornblower") Fanshaw. This consisted of special "pockets" in trousers or greatcoats. The pockets were filled with soil, which was distributed evenly throughout the compound by the wearer. Bernard was one of the "Penguins," as they were called.

The tunnel, called "Harry," was completed by March of 1944, and the first moonless night after this was selected to be the escape day. For the escape, Roger Bushell had paired off with Wing Commander Bob Stanford-Tuck, but the latter was moved to another camp—Beleria—just days before the escape. He then chose Bernard because of the latter's language abilities, and these two were then considered among the seventy escapers most likely to succeed. The pair was chosen to be numbers three and four out of the tunnel.

The day of the Great Escape arrived, and then the problems started! First, the door out from "Harry" was stuck solid, and took an hour to free. Then they found the tunnel had been made twenty feet too short, and ended in the *clearing* outside the fence, rather than in the forest beyond, as had been intended. So, somebody had to go out first and act as a signaller. These delays reduced the expected number of escapers from 200 to 100. Finally the escapes got underway, with the signaller giving the "All Clear."

Once out, and on their way, Bushell and Scheidhauer made their way to the Sagan railway station and caught a train to Breslau. This part was relatively easy, as no alarm had yet been raised that an escape was in progress; and an opportune air raid in the region helped as well (this air raid, however, did not help the escape process itself, as all lights, including those in the tunnel, were doused, making things even slower). The two were seen at Breslau by another escaper, Raymond Van Wymeersch, but neither acknowledged the other's presence. Bushell and Scheidhauer caught another train to Saarbrücken, where their luck ran out.

They were hoping to continue on from there into France. However, they were unfortunately asked to show their papers in the station, and when the papers did not contain a certain mark, the Gestapo was alerted. The jig was finally up when Bernard answered the guard's "Have a good day" by responding in English, "Thank you." They were arrested and turned over to the Gestapo in the form of Obersturmbannführer Dr. Leopold Spann and imprisoned in the local "*Kripo*" prison for several days. Then at Gestapo headquarters, a shocked secretary, Gertrude Schmidt, was ordered by Dr. Spann to type up two death certificates in the names of Bushell and Scheidhauer. When asked by her if they were already dead, Spann said, "Yes, one has just died of appendicitis."

Dr. Spann, with *Kriminalsecretar* Emil Schultz took the two escaped airmen by car, with Gestapo driver Walter Breithaupt, on the road towards Mannheim. Stopping along the way, Dr. Spann took Breithaupt aside and cautioned him to keep his mouth shut about what was to happen to the prisoners, or the same would happen to him. Then he ordered the prisoners out of the car to relieve themselves at the side of the road. As soon as their trouser buttons were undone, they were both shot in the head: Bushell by Schultz, and Scheidhauer by Spann. Bernard was killed immediately, but Roger rolled over, moaning, requiring another bullet in the head from Schultz. The date was March 29th, 1944. The bodies were taken to Nene Bremm concentration camp near Saarbrücken for cremation, and the urns containing the ashes then returned to Sagan for burial. Bushell was thirty-three and Scheidhauer was twenty-two.

Of the seventy-six men who actually escaped through "Harry," fifty were murdered (including Bushell and Scheidhauer), twenty-three were recaptured but survived, and only three made the "home run"—i.e., returned to their home bases in England. The senseless slaughter of these fifty airmen, whose direct order from their own superiors was to try to escape, was unforgivable. The justification given for it, by Germany, was that due to an impending Second Front, every soldier they had was required for defending their frontiers, not for chasing escapers. There was a certain amount of truth in this, because every escaper or evader on the loose requires at least two soldiers to find him. However, shooting them was not one of the requirements, and was hence treated as a war crime.

After the war was over, the search by the British for the assassins of the escaped prisoners resulted in the arrests of Schultz on August 10th, 1945, in a French-controlled concentration camp near Saarbrücken, and Breithaupt on July 10th, 1946, in Frankfurt am Main, and their convictions followed. Schultz was executed by hanging on February 27th, 1948, and Breithaupt sentenced to life imprisonment. Dr. Spann was killed in Linz, Austria, on March 24th, 1945, during one of the final bombing raids of the war by the U.S. Air Force.

With thanks to the following:

Christiane & Francois Magne—Paris, France (the family)
Jean-Loup Niox—Paris, France (the family)
William & Annie Magne—Paris, France (the family)
Maryse McKeon (nee Marniere)—Tampa, Florida (friend of the family)
Roger Huguen—France,"Par les nuits les plus longues" (input)
Ian Le Sueur—Jersey, "Pilot Officer Scheidhauer—The Forced Landing"
and "The Great Escape" (input)
Bert Dowty—Great Britain (input)
Bruce Strand—Innisfail, Alberta, Canada (translations)

Bernard Scheidhauer and his Presentation Spitfire V.

tossed like peas in a can

The Bailout of F/O John Dix, RAF, with #158 Squadron

John was the bomb aimer of a four-engine Halifax bomber, and was flying deep into Germany on his twenty-first operation when his plane was shot down by enemy fighters. In his own words, John tells us about the attack and the bailout:

"A few minutes after the navigator advised us we were approaching the Moselle, I heard several heavy thuds and a change in the roar of the engines. Then a small flaming incendiary shell passed between my legs from behind. It made a neat round hole in the plastic nose dome in front of me, as it passed through, and continued along my line of sight for several seconds. There was a steady clatter from our machine guns in the turrets behind me. The voice of the rear gunner came over the radio in the form of a scream, making a vague reference to an approaching fighter. Then only silence from him and his guns. In the same instant, the pilot called to say that both starboard engines were on fire, and that the aircraft was becoming hard to control.

"I glanced behind me and saw the flight engineer slumped over his control panel, minus his flying helmet, with blood pouring from a wound in his scalp. I realized then that we were in serious trouble. Our gunner in the middle turret called that the fighter now appeared to be firing again from the right side, but with the bomb bays on fire, and the flames from it and the engines, he was prevented from taking aim at the fighter.

"Tracer shells were thudding into our aircraft, and our middle gunner was firing blindly into the night. Our plane was now obviously out of control. While I was being thrown violently against the side of the fuselage, the pilot was shouting over the radio for us to bail out. He had no more control over the plane, which was tossing violently from side to side. The time had more than arrived for us to abandon 'ship.'

"The nose escape hatch was under the navigator's seat and had an emergency handle designed to release it. This was quite difficult, with us being tossed about in the fuselage like peas in a can. But we finally got it open and dropped the door into the night. Our navigator took his position facing the rear, sat down on the edge of the open hatch, gave a quick glance at the two of us waiting, then disappeared in a flash. I caught a momentary glimpse of him as he fell free and shouted to my radioman that the navigator had caught fire. I sat on the edge of the hatch and hesitated for a moment for fear of catching fire myself as I jumped.

Before I had a chance to make up my own mind, a violent swing of the crippled plane threw me bodily out into the night. I received a terrific jolt as I left the plane; my head was wrenched backwards, and helmet and both flying boots were torn off me by the rush of air. My right hand was locked tightly on the release handle of my parachute and I must have pulled it immediately I was thrown from the plane. I received another bone-shaking jolt when my chute opened above me. I lost sight of the furiously burning plane as it plunged earthward.

"For the following few minutes I must have lost consciousness, since my next memory was of a terrible loneliness. The lack of noise was the most striking thing; all I could hear was the faint hum of bombers continuing on their way high above me. I was swaying gently from side to side beneath the huge canopy of my parachute. When I looked up to see it there was a sharp pain in my throat. I instinctively put my hand to the pain and it came away covered with blood. I was too scared to explore my body further, as the thought crossed my mind that my neck was broken. I vomited from shock and fear as I slowly floated down in the darkness.

"I was still swaying very gently from side to side like a pendulum when I glimpsed what appeared to be a small patch of trees flashing by below me. I realized I was moving quite fast across them. Before I could brace myself for the shock of landing, I hit the ground hard and rolled into a heap of soft ploughed earth. My parachute settled softly into a heap beside me."

This story came by way of a personal letter from John Dix, who is now a resident of Canada.

εscape from the Back εnd

The Bailout of P/O Denis Budd, RCAF, of #405 Pathfinder Squadron

The date was August 16th, 1944, and the target of that day's raid was Stettin on the Baltic. They got to the target, marked it, and were headed for home when the attack happened. The story, in Denis's words, is as follows:

"Being a tail gunner, it was awful hard to know where you were, because things were gone before you saw them. I heard this thump, thump, thump, right down the side of the aircraft, and I knew right away that it was anti-aircraft fire. Then a cannon shell came through the bottom of my turret, hit the base of the outside gun, and buggered it up completely. The intercom was out, flames were coming out of the port engine, and then I saw a night fighter coming up from underneath.

"When I realized that the intercom was out, I decided that things were getting too hot and I should get the hell out of there. I had a seat pack instead of the usual chest-type parachute. This was unusual [but was necessary] because there was not much room in the rear turret for a parachute. The chest pack was kept inside the plane, but if I had flown with one of them I wouldn't be alive today.

"I wound the turret around on the beam with the hand crank, got the sliding door open and stuck my ass out, took off my helmet and intercom, and fell out backwards—almost. I got my left leg out all right, but my right leg was jammed between the turret and the body of the plane just above the ankle.

"There I was, hanging upside down outside a burning plane at 18,000 feet! At times like that you get a tremendous rush of energy, so I was able to pull myself up, in spite of hanging backwards in the slipstream. I managed to get to the top of the zipper of the outer flying suit, and I kept wiggling it down inch by inch as far as I could. I kept wiggling my foot out of the boot and finally my foot slipped out, and I broke free. I came down with one boot and a leg as black as the ace of spades.

"On the way down I thought, 'Holy doodle, what if the skipper gets that fire out and he flies home to Britain without a tail gunner. What a fool I'm going to look like, because nobody told me to bail out.' Then I started to think of the craziest things. I used to take a lot of photographs—I had stacks of them at home—and I wondered what would happen to them. Eventually I made a perfect landing with only one boot. I rolled over and was up in a flash and buried my chute in a patch of cabbages."

From a personal communication received from P/O Budd.

I Heard the Angels Call

The Bailout of Flight Sergeant Nicholas Alkemade of the RAF on March 24th, 1944

This is probably the most incredible bailout story ever recorded of a man who fell 18,000 feet without a parachute, and lived to tell about it.

"By closing my eyes, I can experience once again that awful sensation of falling, plunging down into the bottomless pit of night in the frightful three-mile drop from my blazing bomber. I always wake up in a cold sweat just before I hit the ground; and sometimes I reread a worn document that says it was all true, and it happened over Germany on the night of March 24th, 1944.

"With our bombs gone, we were headed home for bacon, eggs, and sleep, when suddenly our Lancaster shuddered with blasts from cannon shells that set us on fire. It was a hopeless situation as the pilot gave the order to bail out. I opened the doors of my rear turret to get the parachute pack, but was met with a wall of searing hot flames. I could see my parachute just beyond my reach, burning. The heat was unbearable as I closed the doors. At that moment, a black shadowy shape of a JU–88 Night Fighter closed in behind us. In desperation, I depressed the Brownings and fired a long burst; I could see the tracers hitting his port engine, which exploded in flames.

"I managed to turn the turret to the side, tore off my helmet and in despair, tumbled out, backwards into space. I felt a strange peace, away from the shrivelling heat, as I plunged towards eternity with the cool air rushing past my face.

"If this was dying, it was nothing to be afraid of, only a pleasant feeling, but with regrets over not saying goodbye to my friends. I blacked out.

"Awareness returned slowly. I was very cold, my arms and legs felt paralyzed as I struggled to sit up. Then it came to me—I'm alive. I ran my hands over my body and limbs as I felt a terrible pain in my back and shoulders, my head throbbed and burns covered my face and legs. I had a twisted knee, a splinter wound in my thigh, and a bad scalp cut.

"I must have crashed down through fir branches and come to a stop in a snowbank in a million-to-one landing. To try and escape in my condition would be very foolish, so I began to blow my whistle; soon, in the distance, I could hear men shouting. A flashlight shone in my face and in brusque German, I was ordered to get up—I shook my head. With that I was hauled to my feet and promptly collapsed in a dead faint. I was later taken to a warm farmhouse where villagers filed in to see what a *Luft* gangster looked like. Later two Gestapo men shoved me into a car and drove [me] to a hospital in a place called Meshede, where my ragged clothes were cut away and I was given medical attention.

"Then began a comic opera interrogation: 'What did you do with your parachute?' I replied that I didn't have one. With that, he slapped me across the face and said, 'Don't be funny, English, where did you bury it?' I could see that he did not believe me but it was the truth, so I told him that it burned up in the plane and I jumped without it. 'That's impossible!' he shouted, and shook me so hard that I passed out again.

"For days, the interrogation continued, until I was taken to *Dulag-Luft* and put in solitary confinement for a week. After a few days the answer came to me in the middle of the night and I finally slept soundly for the first time in weeks. One morning I was taken out to face a Lieutenant Hans Feidal, a *Luftwaffe* officer who spoke perfect English in a quiet voice. He still wanted to know where my parachute was, but I told him the same as I had many times before, that I had jumped without one.

"I could see the anger mounting in him, so I added, 'If you'll bring me the harness I was wearing when you found me, I can prove my story,' and with that he snapped out an order to an orderly. Within a short time he returned with the harness and I buckled it on. Facing the officer, I showed that the hooks and liftwebs were still tied down with thread, just as they were when I jumped out. Had I used a parachute pack, they would have been pulled free. 'Let me see that,' he said, and shook his head in disbelief. The word spread like wildfire. German airmen crowded around as I retold the story, and they laughed and congratulated me on being alive.

"I was marched in front of about 200 Allied prisoners as Lieutenant Feidal asked for the senior British officer to step forward. With that he said, 'I want you to write this down, as it must be a matter of record that this event has been investigated and found to be true.' F/L H.J. Moore tore a blank sheet of paper from a Bible and wrote as the *Luftwaffe* Officer dictated, and [it] was signed by F/L Moore, F/S Lamb and F/S T.A. Jones, 25/4/44.

"All that seems so long ago now and even today I still wonder if it really happened, but when I open my billfold and take out a worn bit of paper, the flyleaf of a Bible, to read those words '. . . the claim of Sergeant Alkemade, 1431537 of the RAF is true in all respects' . . ."

This account is based on tales available from the Internet and other common sources.

It is also very remarkable that this jump occurred on the same night that the Great Escape took place.

16P

2nd Election European Parliament

VE DAY
VE
40TH ANNIVERSARY OF THE
8 MAY 85
BRITISH FORCES POSTAL SERVICES 1945

RAFES SC.36

The Caterpillar Club
commemorating the 40th Anniversary
of the Formation of the
Royal Air Forces Escaping Society

Flown in Hercules C130 MK 1.XV191, Call Sign Ascot 4824 from RAF Lyneham to the International Air Tattoo at Fairford where the covers were carried by members of the RAF Falcons in a delayed parachute descent from 12,000 ft.

Captain:	Flt. Lt. E. Coleman RAF
Co-Pilot:	Flt. Lt. A. Swift RAF
Navigator:	Flt. Lt. A. Judge RAF
Engineer:	Master Engineer C. Smith
Air Loadmaster:	Flt. Sgt. B. Birkin
Flight Time:	20 Minutes

Parachutists:
Flt. Lt. Mike Milburn RAF
Flt. Lt. Derek Warby RAF
Flt. Sgt. Ty Barraclough AFM
Sgt. Rod Crawford
Sgt. Nick Oswald
Sgt. Simon Robert Perry
Sgt. Barry Charnock
Sgt. Mark John Perry
Sgt. Andy Stalker
Sgt. Chris Francis
Sgt. Nick Martin
Sgt. Ken D'Souza

Bomber Command
Museum
Aerodrome Road
Hendon

A Caterpillar Commemoration.

BLESS YOU, *Brother Irvin*

An Aviator's Story

The Bailout of Flt. Sgt. Robert Chester-Master, R.A.A.F. of #514 Squadron

Robert was the rear gunner on a Lancaster III on the night of August 12th, 1944. The target was Rüsselsheim, in southwest Germany, very close to Frankfurt. The flight into the target was fairly normal, and the bombs were dropped on schedule. However, once the plane turned towards their home at Waterbeach, in England, and they picked up speed and dropped down to lower altitudes for a faster trip, that was when the "fun" began. To put it in Mr. Chester-Master's words:

"Flak very heavy, hundreds of searchlights and more bombers hit. Suddenly we are caught in a cone of searchlights and the flak intensifies as the anti-aircraft guns try to get our range. Skillful flying by the Skipper finally gets us out of this dangerous situation. We fly on over Belgium with hope in our hearts when at 0200 hours the attack begins again and this time we are badly hit.

"The port outer motor stops—Skipper feathers the engine—no worries as we have gotten home before on two engines. Mid-upper gunner reports extensive fuel leak from wing tanks and small explosions from the starboard inner, and we are losing height rapidly. Skipper reports hydraulics gone and very little control, so he orders bail out, bail out, and I centralize turret, open the doors, and climb back into the fuselage to clip on my parachute.

"By the time I reached the rear door, it was open, and obviously I was the last one out from this area. Now down to about 700 ft., so I jumped and immediately pulled the rip cord. Usually we would count to seven, so that we would not hit the tailplane—no time for that, and, luckily for me, I dropped quickly and the chute opened minutes before striking terra firma with an awful shock that went right through my body. Intense pain shot up my left leg—so I knew I was in trouble.

"In the short time between bailing out and landing, the stricken plane crashed with a fireball of flame from the petrol, which lit up the night sky. Thoughts raced through my mind: was I the only survivor, or had other crew escaped? The answer was not known until much later. The present questions were: where was I and what time was it? I could only guess at both—somewhere in Belgium, and about 0230 hours, as my watch had been torn from my wrist.

"Now the pain was intense, and sending shafts up my leg, but it would have to wait until light, before I could examine the damage.

"As my eyes became accustomed to the gloom, I realized I was in a field of haystacks, so, gathering the parachute, I clawed my way in. With the chute wrapped around me, I soon fell into an exhausted sleep.

"When I awoke, shafts of light showed through the hay, so I pushed my flying gear further into the stack and crawled out to see the sun well up in the sky. The pain in my leg was intense, so I opened my escape kit and downed some painkillers.

"What was I to do? Here I was, a nineteen-year-old Australian flyer, in a foreign country, unable to speak the language, with what I thought was a broken leg, cold, hungry, thirsty, deep behind enemy lines, and feeling lonely. A feeling of apprehension flooded over me and I felt a surge of self-pity, but I soon realized that this would not help me and I should adopt a more positive attitude—so I resolved to act.

"Undoing my tie and taking out the collar stud, I scraped at the back and this revealed the hidden compass to give me the direction to go; so I resolved to try and walk, hoping to pick up a large stick to help me, as I had realized my leg was not broken, but I had sustained a severely sprained ankle and it appeared that a small bone had been displaced.

"I could see some woods in the distance, and farther away to the side where the plane crashed was a village, so I gave thought to first finding a hiding place in the woods. At that moment, I saw a farmer crossing the field with his dog, which came bounding and barking over to me. This drew the attention of his master, who followed.

"A very difficult attempt at conversation followed, as he spoke Flemish and I spoke only English, but I gathered that he wanted to tell the Germans, who could possibly help me with my leg. This idea didn't 'sit' too well with me, as it was our duty to avoid capture, so I made perfectly plain my rejection. This was not bravado, but a built-in desire not to be incarcerated in a prison camp or something even worse.

"He then pointed to the woods and indicated I should go there and wait—for what? Help, or danger? I had no choice, so I stumbled over and into the woods and sat down exhausted. I guessed the time to be after noon, and by now I was very thirsty and hungry, but decided against using the emergency rations in my escape kit. This consisted of chocolate, sugared almonds, chewing gum, fishing line, pocketknife, Benzedrine tablets, and tablets for cleansing water, as well as French, Belgian, and Dutch money.

"Evening drew on, and I made a bed in the bracken, but spent a restless night, thinking that every sound is a German searching for me.

"Morning came, and I heard a low whistle from the edge of the woods. I stumbled out to find food and water, but no person; at least I am safe for the moment. The day dragged by—evening came—another whistle in the morning and food again.

"The third day, two men came from another direction; a smattering of English to indicate 'friends,' and they would be back. All I could do now was wait—my leg still ached and I guess I was falling into a morbid state. The next morning, the two men returned quite early and the bigger one lifted me on his back, and I was on my way."

Robert's fall was only about 700 feet, but this height is considered about the minimum for a safe bailout. With an initial velocity of about thirty-two feet/sec, and acceleration of thirty-two feet/sec/sec, he would have under twenty seconds to avoid hitting the ground full on. How thankful I am for my almost 900 seconds!

In order to fully appreciate the bailout predicament of Robert Chester-Master's crew, the action as seen by another member of his crew goes as follows:

"In the tail turret, Chesty saw a stream of green tracers suddenly streak towards him from about three hundred yards, starboard quarter, eleven o'clock high.

"He suddenly became very active. Sam's turret was to the port after a sweep that way, but he heard the yell and saw streaks of green go past and arc slowly away.

"'Fighter—corkscrew starboard, go!'

"As Chesty yelled, he was already moving his guns. With a speed difference of perhaps 30 mph, at three hundred yards, the gunners would have perhaps ten seconds to return fire. The attacker broke to port quarter down—below, to Chesty's right. Having tracked back the tracer line and followed the attacker, he could identify it as it banked; a Junkers 88.

"John Lawrie hurled the unladen Lancaster to starboard and down, as Sam swung his turret from port beam towards the source of the tracer, which had swept overhead to rake across the wings and fuselage from right to left. Chesty was already firing—the corkscrew might add a second or two to the time that both gunners could engage the fighter. He saw flames jet from the starboard engine of the Ju–88, and Sam saw his own tracer fly towards the German fighter and strike it as it dived away.

"As he swung G-George to port, following the manoeuvre through, John Lawrie wondered where the hits had been—they were audible enough. He wrestled with the control column, without the benefit of any form of power assistance, continuing evasive action. The fighter seemed to have gone, which was just as well. The kite didn't feel right. One by one the crew called in; at least something was in one piece.

"As he panted into his mask, straining with the sluggish controls, he heard Sam, the mid-upper: 'Skipper . . . starboard inner's hit, it's on fire.'

"John glanced at the flight engineer, 'Feather it, Tommy. This kite flies like a bloody brick.' It was still possible that they would make it home, but he ordered chutes on all round. G-George had taken hits across both wings. But by some miracle, only one shot could be found, which had hit in the forward fuselage, and it had caused no injury. Just then the two port engines failed. Down to two thousand feet, and bloody hard to control, and the hydraulics gone, it was questionable how much time they had left in the air at all. Now down to a thousand feet.

"'Skipper to crew: Bail out, Bail out . . .' Martin Carter (bomb aimer) twisted the latch of the forward escape hatch, and jumped. Tom Young (flight engineer) followed, and then finally Reg Orth (navigator) jumped through the nose hatch.

"Hopefully John Lawrie (pilot) would follow. Further back, the tail door had been whipped away by the slipstream. Sam Burford (mid-upper gunner) tumbled out, followed by George Durland (wireless operator). Chesty was last; he had some difficulty fixing his chute in place, and had decided that if there was a time to feel scared, then that time had arrived.

"G-George was down to 700 feet! Six crewmembers had made it out alive, but with a mixed bag of safety. Most of them were alive, if not unscathed.

"Later when the wreck of the crashed Lancaster was searched, a charred parachute pack lay in the grass nearby. As the bomber did not carry spare parachutes, the pack had to be that of the pilot, John Lawrie.

"'*He Shall Grow Not Old*'—*Part of the Tribute to the war dead.*"

This story was received by mail from Robert Chester-Master, now living in Brisbane, Australia, and a member of the Australian Caterpillar Club.

The sharks, the crocs, and the Japs

The Escape of F/Sgt D.J. Barnett, RAAF, over Burma on February 26th, 1943

"**I** was flying No. 2 to Warrant Officer Bing De Cruyenaere on Blenheim Bomber escort, to targets just north of Akyab Island. We were top cover of three sections of Hurricane fighters. Such was the jungle camouflage of the bombers and our fighter aircraft, it was not possible with only six aircraft to have safe height advantage from enemy fighter attack and still keep visual contact.

"Bing and I were at about 8,000 feet when I was shot down. So severe were the strikes on my Hurricane, I believed it was Japanese heavy anti-aircraft fire from Akyab Base until confirming that it was fighter interception on my return to the squadron.

"Akyab Island was the main Japanese coastal base above Rangoon. Impression remains of loud explosions and smoke, the strong stench of fire and explosives, gaping holes in the cockpit emergency panel on my right, smashed instrument panel, stopped engine, and the aircraft violently spinning. The cockpit filled with smoke, I recall, as the spin tightened. I had to get out on the inside of the spin, and, in a dazed way, I felt this was the end of me and my war.

"Releasing hood and safety straps, I recall the slipstream wrenching me from the cockpit and then I was tumbling downwards, grasping for the rip cord handle without success. But then I was easily able to look down my body and place my hand on the release to the parachute, and pull. From my then floating parachute, I could follow a great trail of smoke to my poor aircraft now burning furiously a few hundred yards in from the shore of the island. Tearing away north were my Hurricane mates, and my isolation and loneliness were extreme.

"Above me, but hidden by the vast white canopy of the chute, were the Japanese fighters, as evidenced by their loud engine noises. That I could be easily seen was undoubted, and that I'd be riddled with bullets was fairly certain. Beyond this was the overwhelming fear of how I would stand up as a prisoner to these Japanese, when our intelligence had told us so much about their utmost brutalities. I asked for God's courage to face what was ahead of me.

"Like a wonderful cloak, courage-belief was given to me; a full belief that I would manage. This miracle stays with me to this day. I spilled air from my chute in an effort to keep off the shore and away from the large gathering of natives gazing and waving at me from the gray beach. I clearly saw a row of posts in the water, probably barbed-wire anti-landing defenses. When it appeared I should fall into the water some three hundred yards from the shore, I inflated my Mae West.

"Somehow, as I hit the water, I banged the parachute quick release, scrambling and treading water to release and inflate the rubber dinghy that had been the seat to my chute. It was all very difficult, since I had never done any of this before with my life depending on it. I struggled with the pin locking the oxygen bottle, almost screwing the knob from the bottle in desperation. But the dinghy inflated perfectly, and a huge yellow thing appeared. I was not going to be as small and unseen as I wanted to be at this time.

But at least I was down to earth in Burma, even if it was less than solid earth.

"As the tide carried me and my half-filled dinghy along parallel to the beach, the inhabitants followed me, calling in a language I could not understand, while a couple of Jap fighters patrolled overhead with probably more a swag higher. Having lost the paddles, I propelled the dinghy by hand towards some mangroves some two miles away. Other than the dinghy, all I had were a tin of mosquito cream, an empty water bag, a revolver and ammunition, and some 150 rupees in cash."

Once Barnett reached the so-called haven of the mangrove trees, his story then continued on until he was safely back in friendly territory. However, along the way he had to contend with some very dicey situations, which included the infamous Mugger crocodiles, sharks, friendly and unfriendly natives, the Japanese, who were searching for him, the wet jungle he traversed, the Mayu river he had to swim, and a very suspicious British sentry when he thought he had finally reached friendly territory.

F/Sgt. Barnett's story, including both his achievement of Caterpillar status and his return home from the landing spot, make me glad my bailout was in relatively "quiet" France. German fighters and unfriendly natives I can take, but Mugger crocs and sharks? No thanks!

A Matter of circumstance

The Story of P/O Lionel Rackley, Pilot of the RAAF

At first sight, it would have seemed that the bailout by Lionel Rackley was perfect, given all the circumstances surrounding it. After all, he had already lived through two crashes in his air force career, and hence felt immune. Even the bailout itself was made over friendly territory, after their crippled Lancaster had made it back to England. His parachute pack was untouched, even after all the garbage thrown at the plane by the unseen enemy. Everything pointed towards a nice, soft landing, and an early return to base.

But circumstances have a way of "mucking up" the best-laid hopes of flyers, especially when they are trying to escape by parachute.

On June 21st/22nd of 1944, on the way to bomb Wesseling, a German night fighter, using the "*Schlage Musik*" method of attack, made mincemeat of their control systems. However, with what they had left, and enough engine power, the crew made their way back to England. But with no way to land the plane, it was decided they must bail out. Below them was safety—or so they thought.

The first sign of problems came when they found that the parachute of the rear-gunner had been ruined during the attack. The bomb-aimer volunteered to take the gunner with him, using only his chute, and so they were tied together with ropes. Holding one another face-to-face, they were launched through the forward escape hatch. Unfortunately, when the chute opened, the ropes broke, and the gunner fell away. He was killed, but the bomb-aimer landed safely and was awarded the British Empire Medal for his effort.

After this, the rest of the crew jumped until only Lionel Rackley, the pilot, was left. By now the plane was uncontrollable, so he crawled to the front escape hatch, rolled himself up, and left the plane head first, in the prescribed manner. Counting up to five, and turning head-over-heels with a view of the wing-tip lights at each turn, he pulled the rip cord. The chute opened and the exhilaration of free fall ceased. He was now floating towards earth. Lionel had lost a flying boot during the fall, and he tucked the unshod cold foot into his remaining boot for some warmth. A nice, soft landing was the next order of business.

But then he heard the noise of aircraft engines approaching, and out of the darkness of early morning his Lancaster, flying at a crazy angle, passed some distance above him. The noise diminished for a few moments and then came again, and the aircraft, in an even tighter turn, passed beneath him. Lionel heaved a sigh of relief when he realized the danger of collision with the aircraft had passed—it had been a horrible few moments. The sounds of the engines was heard for some time, and suddenly an orange glow lit the clouds below, followed by the sound of an almighty explosion. Fortunately, the plane had landed in open country, and no injuries were caused by the crash.

Far below him he could see the tops of clouds, but it did not seem they were getting any closer; the darkness of the early morning made it difficult for him to tell if he was being carried upwards or downwards. But eventually he reached the clouds and started through. However, the cloud base must have been extremely low, because no sooner had Lionel hit them than he was through, and encountering his next obstacle to a soft landing.

Immediately after passing through the clouds, he realized that he was being dragged along at a terrific rate and became aware of the distinctive sounds made by train wheels, rattling beside his ear. He was being bumped about quite violently, but felt little pain or fear. Lionel felt very little else until suddenly he found himself walking along a railroad line. His second flying boot, his watch, and his chute were all gone. And so was the train.

Instead of the nice, soft, ground, as many newly initiated "Caterpillars" hoped for, Lionel Rackley had hit a train! Picking up the chute, the train had started to drag him along, but unfortunately the quick-release mechanism had been smashed. The train ripped the parachute from Lionel's body, leaving him lying beside the track.

He heard later that when the train arrived in one of the London stations—Waterloo—with the parachute still entangled, it created quite a stir among the passengers and railroad staff. Locomotives do not normally carry parachutes!

From a personal communication of the Caterpillar Club of Australia.

ınto the cɑuldron

The Bailout of F/O John Neal, RCAF, on April 22nd, 1944

The attack came without any warning at all. One moment I was leaning over my bombsight, the release button in my right hand, and just about to perform the most accurate bombing of my career. At 6,000 feet, on a clear night, with target indicators lighting up everything, who could miss those rail yards?

But the next moment came the sudden explosions and flashes of light that ruined everything. We were hit, and almost directly over the target of the night. I did a quick check to see that there were no wounds on my body, and then rushed up to the cockpit to see how the others, and the plane, had fared.

The plane was on fire in both port engines and a part of the fuselage. We had been caught napping by a German night fighter, quite possibly from below, where he couldn't be seen. Chuck Thomas, our pilot, had been wounded in the attack, but obviously not seriously enough to hamper his handling of the controls. He was turning the plane north to get away from the target area. When I asked for instructions, his reply was to "Get the hell out!"

I took this for the bailout order, and started to return to my nose position.

Suddenly remembering all those live, high-explosive bombs that were still on board, I shouted back to Chuck, "Hold everybody a minute. Let me get the bombs away first." Going up front, I set all the bombs on "safe" and pushed the jettison button. Without another thought, I strapped my parachute pack onto the chest hooks of my harness and turned to the nose escape hatch.

It took a bit of pushing and kicking, but finally the door dropped away into the night. Bob Lindsay jumped first, and, as soon as he had disappeared, I sat down on the edge of the hatch getting ready to go. The last person I saw in the plane was Pat Murphy, blood streaming down his face, yelling, "Get out, get out!" I pushed myself outwards and let go the edge. Then I found that I had pushed too hard; I hit the opposite side of the hatch and slid straight down. My jaw collided with the edge, and this gave me an aching chin, which lasted for weeks after. However, I fell, otherwise safely, away from the plane, and almost immediately pulled the rip cord on my parachute. There was the initial jerk of the straps, and very shortly I found myself floating earthward with a fully opened canopy.

So far, in my air force career, I had not been able to give too much thought to the act of "bailing out," but I had just done it! Our only training was verbal, but of course we were all confident that we would never be called on to use the training. Now on a night that was as black as the pits of hell, all I could see, while hanging from the shroud lines, was one plane, in flames, moving rapidly away from me.

However, the flames were probably not big enough for the *Luftwaffe* pilot. Seeking to make certain of his "kill," he flew on after our Halifax, passing within a few yards of my parachute in the process. This set up a rather fierce swaying that carried on for several minutes and scared the hell out of me. Then just as the swaying started to ease off, somebody in the bomber stream hit an ammunition train! Having bailed out only a couple of miles from the target area, I now had a box seat for this fireworks display. Then I started to hear shrapnel from the explosions whistling by. There is not a lot one can do to reduce oneself in size in a parachute, but what I did must have succeeded. All of the shrapnel whizzed safely by, so it must have been a pretty big sky I was in.

And then, suddenly, I hit the ground! I had not expected it quite so soon, but from 6,000 feet, I should have known that it wouldn't take very long. And on such a dark night, I had no hope of seeing what I was coming down to. But again my luck was holding; I did land on the most ideal of landing spots. It was a soft, just-plowed field. There were a few stars created by the landing, but these quickly disappeared. Gathering up my parachute, I sat down to think about my new situation for a while. I was a stranger, in a strange land, and with no immediate ideas of what to do or where to go.

Even then, I was not able to do very much thinking. The shrapnel continued to fly past overhead. In order to reduce myself as an available target, I was forced to lie prostrate for some time. Finally the raid was over, and the survivors headed for home. Then came the first opportunity for me to experience loneliness. What was I going to do now and in which direction would I go?

The suggested route, given to us by headquarters, was towards Paris, and to seek help along the way. More Resistance people were operating out of Paris than anywhere else, so our chances of help there were greatest. I checked my small button compass and prepared to set out in a southwesterly direction towards the capital city.

But then the voices started up! They were very close by, but I could not tell in which language they were speaking. Another half-hour passed before they faded away, and it was again clear for my departure. They had probably been French, since I would have been easy to find had they been Germans searching for me. They could not have been more than twenty or thirty feet away. The tone of the voices seemed to indicate an amorous liaison, rather than a searching one. Then I buried my parachute and harness in the earth of my field, tossed the Mae West into a copse of trees nearby, and set off walking towards Paris.

What happened after I started walking can be read in my book *The Lucky Pigeon*. The site of my bailout is shown on page 69, in a map amended by Eddie Lee Rosier of Paris, France. The

BLESS YOU, *Brother Irvin*

map shows the direction of my attack, the target of Laon, and, ten kilometres north of the target, my landing place. The reader might note where the name "Cauldron" came from, with the presence of several High Nazi retreats and a fair number German Army units and *Luftwaffe* airports in the area.

The author at nineteen years of age.

The casualty Report

Reports by the Members of the Crew of F/O John A. Neal

Except in the case of the flyers who have to bail out of a single-seater fighter plane, Caterpillars seldom join the club by themselves. They mainly form a part of a crew numbering from two to ten or more. When a plane such as a Flying Fortress is shot down, up to ten parachutes will be seen if, as we would hope, all the crew escape. Should several B–17s be destroyed at the same time, the resulting escapes could resemble a paratrooper invasion!

Most fortunately, by flying by night, the planes of RAF Bomber Command did not offer such a spectacle when they were shot down, nor did they contribute the same number of new members to the club. These planes carried seven crewmembers, while the B–17s carried ten. Twin-engined planes carried two to five men in their crew.

Not all of these men were able to parachute safely to the ground; many were killed in the attacks, many lost their parachutes to fire, and, sadly, many were unable to open their chutes after jumping. Only a few tried to jump without a parachute, and we have some of the few to succeed, and live, including F/Sgt Nicholas Alkemande.

But the stories of the escapes, as told by the different members of the same plane, show some of the conditions during this time of stress. Conditions vary according to who is giving the report. In the case of the author, there were five other members of the crew who bailed out and became Caterpillars (the last was the rear gunner, who, sadly, was killed during the attack). Excerpts from their official reports show somewhat different versions of the same attack.

Common to all Reports

Squadron: 419
Base: Middleton St. George
Aircraft type: Halifax V, No. HX–189, Letter: J
Special Equipment: GEE, H2S, Fishpond
Bomb Load: All High Explosive.
Takeoff time: 2130 hrs.
Target: Laon
Date of Loss: 22/23.4.44
Cause of Loss: Fighter Attack

Remainder of Crew

NAME	RANK	DUTY EXPERIENCE	FATE
Thomas C.	2nd Lt. USAAF Pilot	3	Evader
Lindsay R.P.	Flight Sergeant, Nav.	1	Evader
Neal J.A.	Flying Officer B/A	12	Safe
Murphy P.J.	Warrant Officer W/OP	1	POW
Greene A.	Sgt M/U/G	1	Evader
Knox V.	Sgt R/G	1	Killed
Thompson J.	Sgt F/E	1	POW

C. Thomas, W.A. Greene: Joint Narrative

"The Halifax took off from Middleton St. George at 2036 hours. The French coast was crossed at 10,000 feet, and the target approached at 6,000 feet. About four minutes before reaching the target, flares were seen ahead at about 8,000 feet, and at the same time flak was bursting a few hundred yards away to starboard. There was no moon and visibility was moderate.

"When on the bombing run, the mid-upper gunner saw from the tail blister a Ju–88 outlined against the flares, ten degrees off the tail, at a hundred yards range and fifty feet below. He started to report it, but the rear gunner called out, 'There's a kite on our tail, corkscrew port.' The fighter closed in to fifty yards, firing all the time, but the rear gunner got in first and the mid-upper gunner saw strikes on the enemy's port motor and 'tracer clustering around the nose.' A fire started below the enemy's port motor and an informant claims to have seen it go down and crash in flames.

"The Halifax was hit also, and the flight engineer reported a fire in the port inner engine. The bomb doors were open and bombs on board at the time. The captain, who had not heard the gunner's warning, executed a moderate corkscrew, and turned northward. He then cut the port inner engine, but was unable to feather the propeller; he operated the extinguisher, but it had no effect on the fire.

"About a minute after turning off the track, bombs were jettisoned, but the captain does not recall whether the bomb doors were closed. Meanwhile, a second attack was apparently made from astern as the rear gunner again opened fire; the mid-upper gunner heard bullets strike the fuselage above his head and all the forward part, and saw a fire start in the under part of the starboard wing. The engineer did not report the damage caused in this second attack, which severed the intercom system, but the pilot states that it was more serious than the first. The tail plane was hit and the aircraft tended to dive to port, so the captain increased boost to 46, res 2850. A fire started amidships, but the mid-upper gunner managed to kick it out with his flying boot. The captain had two skin wounds in his left side, and the back of the mid-upper gunner's head was grazed by shell splinters.

"About two minutes after the initial attack, when height was about 5,000 feet, the captain ordered the crew to bail out. Those in the front were instructed verbally; the gunners were called by light signal, but did not reply. All except the rear gunner left by the front exit; the navigator, air bomber, wireless operator, flight engineer and mid-upper gunner had all jumped about a minute after the order was given. The pilot remained in the aircraft a couple of minutes, diving and climbing in the hope of putting out the fires, but the starboard wing and port inner engine were blazing fiercely. He bailed out from about 4,500 feet. It is not known whether the rear gunner bailed out. The captain saw the Halifax crash and explode four miles northeast of Laon, and he landed about one mile west of the aircraft. The mid-upper gunner landed in the target area, and the raid continued for half an hour after he landed."

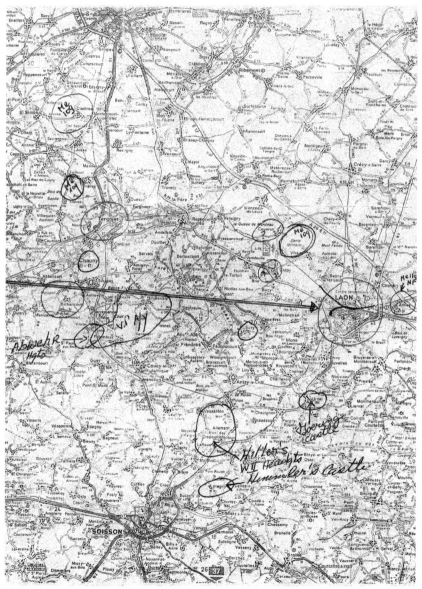

The author's map of the bombing run to Laon.

R.P. Lindsay's Narrative

"Approaching target on bomb-run. Attacked just before bombing. R/G yelled, then a/c hit at once and intercom failed. W/OP said, 'bail out,' he being wounded. Pilot said, 'bail out at once.' Nav. went out first, hatch stuck only a little. Feet first, he bailed out O.K. Height 6000 feet. A/C was shuddering but otherwise under control. Two port engines were on fire. No time to try to put them out. B/A followed him out, landed O.K. Nav. slightly wounded in leg by m.g. bullet. Also nearly hit by S/E fighter in air (not same one probably). Dark moonless clear night. Landed three miles north of Laon."

P.J. Murphy's Narrative

"We took off at approx. 2039 hrs. in a Halifax J with bomb load of H.E. We climbed to a height of approx. 8,000 ft. and set course for the Wash. We crossed the channel and over Belgium on to our target, Laon.

"The radio was working perfect and Group Broadcasts came thru like a bell. I was informed by the skipper we were about to start our bombing run, so I reeled in my TAZI and waited. We seemed to be the first aircraft over the target. We were now flying at 6,000 ft. After the B/A announced 'Bombs gone,' the rear gunner announced 'There is a kite directly behind us.' Then the fighter opened up on us. The radio blew up and the I/C went U/S. I stood up alongside the skipper and he told me to prepare to bail out, which I did. He informed the Nav. and B/A of our trouble, and we managed to open the escape hatch. The B/A bailed out first, Nav. second, and myself third. Difficult to open hatch, jettisoned cover."

J.D. Thompson's Narrative

"Base Middleton St. George. We took off at 9:30 p.m., the weather good. Over target brilliant moon after bombs dropped, sudden burst of cannon fire and I saw JU–88 climbing above us. Pilot asked for chute and then gave order to bail out. Order given by word of mouth, as intercom damaged. Followed W/OP out. Chute worked O.K. and landed safely. R/G had seen enemy a/c approaching about thirty seconds before attack."

All reports are from official RCAF interrogations made after the evasions or prisoner-of-war times were complete.

the triple threat

The Many Bailouts of S/L Gordon Carter, DFC & Bar, of the RCAF

Gordon Carter could be considered a triple threat by any stretch of the imagination, especially during his life in the air force. Firstly, he offered a multi-national background that would make any observer wonder about which country Gordon was really fighting for. Born in France, a citizen of the United Kingdom, educated in the United States, and flying with the Royal Canadian Air Force, he did offer a little bit of each to his war effort.

Even his time in a prison camp in Germany could be considered as a fifth nationality for his overall effort (perhaps Scotland during training could also be thrown in for good measure to assuage the nationalist movement there). Then Gordon decided that one bailout was not enough, so he did it three times. However, even these bailouts had to be over three different countries: France, Britain, and Germany. Compounding this puzzlement, each of the bailouts had to be at different altitudes: the first at 10,000 feet, the second at 1,200 feet, and the third at 23,000 feet.

Talk about keeping the enemy confused! Most of us Caterpillars had to be content with our one encounter with the D-string, but

Gordon must have had the *Luftwaffe* wondering if he would ever stay down. However, he entered into some very auspicious company: that of Charles Lindberg, who had done four; and General Doolittle, who also had done three.

The first landing, the night of February 13th, 1943, took Gordon and his crew to Lorient on the east coast of France. They were to bomb the U-boat pens located there in the campaign to reduce the shipping losses in the Atlantic. Right after dropping their bombs, the plane was hit by some 88mm flak fire, and the plane caught fire. They were at 10,000 feet, and the order to bail out came after attempts to put out the fire. Gordon's description of his jump follows:

"The navigator going first, I snapped back my folding table and seat, clipped my parachute pack onto my harness, removed the hatch in the floor beneath me, and sat on the forward edge of the open hatch with my legs dangling out. Right away the slipstream whipped off one of my flying boots. Then I acknowledged the order to bail out, and only in time did I remember to wrench off my flying helmet, and thus save my head from being torn off.

"I clutched the rip cord handle with my right hand, released the grip I had with my left hand on the opposite rim of the hatch, and with my guts cramped with fear, vanished into 10,000 feet of pitch-black void. I saw the tailfin flash by, pulled the rip cord, and was instantly jerked into immobility by the open chute. After a short moment of the worst anguish I have ever known in my life, I was suddenly totally delivered of it, swinging softly and silently in the pale moonlight.

"As I neared the ground, I heard a voice calling out, and I shouted back, although I have no idea of what I said. I plunged into the arms of a young lad, whose immediate words were, '*Tu est mon frère*' ('You are my brother'). We were in a ploughed field and he collected my chute and led me to a nearby stone farmhouse."

Thus ends the story of Gordon's first bailout, but by no means the end of his relationship with the region. Apparently his evasion included meeting one young lady named Janine, which resulted in a return after the war, and a refusal to leave this time.

Gordon's second jump was about ten months later, after he had returned from France from his first. By then he was on his forty-fifth operation, and on December 20th went to Frankfurt in Germany. The target was bombed and their plane started back home. On their approach, and at 1,200 feet of altitude over England, a target indicator that had hung up in the bomb bay exploded. The plane filled with smoke and flames, and the order to bail out was given immediately.

Gordon obeyed the order, post haste, and was the first out. His chute opened instantly, he saw a tree pass him upside down, and then he hit a ploughed field. This field turned out to be just beyond the perimeter track of his own airfield. A second safe landing, but with a lot less margin for error than the first.

He did not need an evasion this time to get back on ops; he just needed an insensitive commanding officer to send him back on operations the very same day, so he would avoid a "mental blockage against flying."

Gordon's third bailout, and fortunately his last, was over Germany, the one place nobody wanted to visit unless there was a clear route home. Unfortunately for Gordon there was not, and it cost him the balance of the war in a POW camp.

The target was Leipzig, deep in eastern Germany. The date was February 19th, 1944, and, with the distance they would have to fly, the operation was going to be "No piece of cake!" The German fighters started their attacks before they had a chance to cross the coast, and continued for several hours, along with the weaving of Gordon's plane to avoid them. Finally the luck ran out, and they were hit by a JU-88 twin-engine fighter at 0243 hours.

A fuel tank exploded and the plane caught fire. With no chance to extinguish the flames, and the average survival time of a burning plane being thirty seconds, the order for immediate bailout was given. As in the previous two bailouts, the navigator (Gordon) was the first out, after fighting the severe centrifugal forces of a plane spinning out of control. The parachute opened successfully, and he was relieved to find himself alive, even if he was over enemy territory.

This relief took two forms; he was alive, and he was immediately "Off Ops," which also relieved him from asking to be taken off, after all he had been through. The disgrace of "LMF" (Lack of Moral Fibre) was often the reward for those who asked. The balance of the descent was a bit "dicey," as their cruising altitude was 23,000 feet and the temperature at -50 degrees. Compounding the height and the cold was the fact that he had to fall all the way through the bomber stream. Being a member of the Pathfinders, and in the lead, there were a lot of other planes (1,000 in that raid) to fall though. Fortunately he managed to evade them all as they passed to continue on to the target.

Then Gordon started to worry about what awaited him below, which was obscured by complete cloud cover. Knowing he was over hostile territory, he jettisoned his only protection: his revolver. This is of dubious value when one is surrounded by members of the Wehrmacht or a group of irate civilians. Then after about twenty minutes, he spotted a patch of woods with a path running through it; a little manoeuvring with the chute cords and he side-slipped onto the snow-covered path. He did not touch one of the branches of any of the trees (which probably speaks volumes about his talents, after all those other jumps).

After hiding his chute and battledress in the undergrowth, Gordon donned civilian dress and struck out west along the path. His evasion this time was short-lived.

After the war was over, and Gordon was liberated from the POW camp, he returned to France, where he married Janine Jouanjean and has lived in Brittany ever since. It is unfortunate that somebody of authority did not convince Gordon and Janine to emigrate to Canada once the war was over. Canada has plenty of brave warriors from wars past, but is woefully short of Triple Caterpillars.

Main sources: Memoirs of Gordon Carter, *with permission, and* Silent Heroes, Downed Airmen and the French Resistance, *by Sherri Greene Ottis.*

The Test-flight Escape

Most of the previous stories have something to do with the actions of an enemy making necessary the escapes made by parachute. However, long experience has shown that escapes can become necessary even during the tamest of test, training, or pleasure flights. Sometimes our planes just let us down, even without any help from over-eager enemies.

Such a story is that of Mr. James Steel, test pilot for Handley-Page Aircraft Company of England. Test-flying a Halifax on September 23rd, 1943, the following events occurred, and a new Caterpillar was born.

"We took off from Hucknall at 1430 hours, intending to climb to 20,000 feet. I was taking readings of the temperatures at various heights. Mr. Turner, the pilot, was telling me as we reached different heights. Everything appeared normal, and the last reading I took was at 16,000 feet. Mr. Turner then asked me why the red light of the undercarriage was not lit, and I replied that the undercarriage hand-operated up lock must be operated before the light would appear.

"He asked me to try this, and I moved aft to the rest seat and operated the locks; he said this was O.K., and I informed him that I was moving forward to the engineer's panel, leaving the locks off. When I reached this position, I looked through the astrodome and saw that the port outboard engine was on fire. Flames were coming through a hole in the cowling at the top right-hand rear corner, and inside the engine seemed to be burning furiously. I informed the pilot immediately, and he ordered me to stand by for bailing out.

"I clipped on my parachute and looked through the astro hatch again; flames were now shooting through the hole in the cowling. An explosion occurred inside the engine and pieces of cowling fell off. I also noticed that petrol was pouring from the inner vent and the top surface of the intermediate plane. The pilot ordered me to operate the feathering switch; I replied that I could not reach this, as the second pilot's seat was still in the up position. He then ordered me to get the seat down, which I did.

"I then moved forward to the navigator's compartment and opened the front hatch and jettisoned the door. I stood by for bailing out. I glanced through the navigator's window and saw that the port outboard engine was now well alight, and flames were shooting over the wing. I then bailed out at 14,000 feet and landed softly back in England, no worse for the wear and tear."

From communication with Barbara Steel, daughter of Mr. James Steel.

Destiny's Tot

The Bailout of 2nd Lt. Louis Feingold on December 30th, 1943

Lt. Feingold was a navigator on a B-17 Flying Fortress, *Destiny's Tot*, of 336th Squadron, 95th Bomb Group, on a bombing raid to Ludwigshafen, Germany, on December 30th, 1943. After successfully bombing the primary target, his plane was forced to leave the bomb group's formation because of battle damage sustained over the target. He was than attacked by several German fighters. Further crippling damage was sustained, and the crew had no alternative but to bail out.[1]

"When I saw the bombardier zoom past my head, I turned and pulled off my oxygen mask and inter-phone wires. I started out after him feet first. The slipstream caught my legs and I decided that it was best to go out head first as instructed. I had quite a struggle to pull my feet in, but I finally succeeded. The co-pilot was waiting by the hatch when I went out. I had my hand on the rip cord as I dived. I pulled it, but the chute did not open. I must not have pulled it far enough, for when I pulled a second time the chute billowed out and

---

1 From the story, "The Way It Was."

opened smoothly without a jerk. I could see the aircraft. Fighters circled our chutes, and then we started through the overcast. When I came out I could see a chute below me, and a car that was just stopping.

"I hit the ground hard and fell flat on my face. I tried to get up, but my chute started to drag me. I lay still and it stopped, but whenever I tried to move, it would drag me again. I decided that I would have more control if I remained seated. I unhooked the leg straps first, then the chest straps, and got out of my harness. I rolled up the chute and ran with it to a haystack. The straw was too tightly packed for me to be able to make a hole, so I placed the chute on the ground beside the rick. I put my Mae West and helmet on top of the chute and then sat down to rest for a minute. When I had my wind I got up and looked around to see what was going on about me.

"Some peasants were coming towards me. I had started in their direction when I heard someone calling me. I turned around and was joined by Lt. Tarkington.[2]

"From that moment we were taken into the care of the peasants, who handed us over to the French Resistance and we became evaders."

2 From official E & E Report 419–420.

The wedding Dress

A parachute carried by plane from England during a raid on Germany turned into a beautiful wedding dress presently on show in Western Canada.

This is not a normal Caterpillar story where the aviator carrying it was forced to evacuate the plane in order to save his life while it was still flying. This is more the story of the parachute itself and how it changed from an instrument of safety to become a thing of beauty. In fact, it is not even certain who the flyer was that carried the chute to the plane.

It was February 22nd, 1945, and the 392nd Bomb Group, of the 8th Air Force, United States Army Air Force, was assigned to perform low-level attacks on targets in Germany. On this day, the target was the Northeim Marshalling Yards, and the height was 6,000 feet. At this stage in the war, it was more of a terror raid than the heavy bombing that had gone on since 1942. Flying B-24 Liberators, the 392nd took off in late morning, and by mid-afternoon the survivors were on their way back home.

One of the participants of this raid was the *Jolly Duck*, piloted by 1st Lt. Joseph R. Walker. With Walker were eight additional crewmembers manning other positions on the plane, with a staff sergeant, Elmer E. Duerr, holding down the tail gun position. While it is as yet unconfirmed, it is speculated that Sgt. Duerr was instrumental in starting the parachute on its way to wedding dress fame.

The *Jolly Duck* had completed her mission over Northeim and was heading home to base in England. Near Amsterdam, the flight encountered some accurate anti-aircraft fire during which Joe Walker lost an engine. Also, it seems, he lost much of his remaining fuel. They no longer had enough to safely cross the English Channel and get home. While desperately trying to make liberated territory, Lt. Walker was finally forced to crash land in the country near the German-occupied Dutch village of Zoeterwoude. Extensively damaged, the plane came to rest beside the farm of Tinus Janson, a local farmer.

While the plane was damaged, all of the nine crewmembers were able to disembark without any serious injuries. Farmer Janson had seen the crash, as had many of his neighbours who gathered around the site to offer help. One of them was Wilhelm Van Niekerk, a young lad from the region. Suddenly, one of the escaping airmen (perhaps Elmer [Bud] Duerr) came up to Wilhelm and handed him his parachute (which would have been an encumbrance during his escape to freedom).

Figuring that the parachute was just a mass of fabric that would be of little use to him, Van Niekerk later gave it to his girlfriend, Wilhelmina Vanden Berg, who stowed it away until the war was over. Then when the couple decided to get married, Wilhelmina, an expert with the needle, decided to use the parachute fabric to make her wedding dress.

The dress was a wonder to behold, especially during those days of shortage of all materials for this use. When the couple had children, the surplus parachute fabric went into a christening dress for them. It is even rumored that Wilhelm wore nylon underwear made from the parachute!

Years later, the couple immigrated to Canada and brought the dress with them. On March 6th, 2002, the dress was presented to the Aero Space Museum of Calgary to be permanently displayed, and as a thank you for Canada's part in liberating the Netherlands. It now enjoys a prominent place in the museum, as shown in the following picture.

L–R: Fanny Duerr, Wilhelm Van Niekerk, Wilhelmina Van Niekerk; and The Wedding Dress.

The presidential Bailout

The Day That Lt (JG) George Bush Jumped from his Aircraft over the South Pacific

In January of 1993, President George Herbert Walker Bush abandoned his position as the forty-first president of the United States of America in favour of Bill Clinton, the forty-second. George Bush was most likely to have been the final head of state to have also served in World War II. He was a pilot with the U.S. Navy, and, at one time, probably the youngest pilot they had.

But the parachute George Bush received in 1993—the presidential pension—was a lot more likely to promote his future life than did the one he received in 1944.

On February 6th, 1944, Bush, as a graduate pilot, with the wings on his chest, reported to the U.S. light attack carrier, USS *San Jacinto*, flying Avenger torpedo bombers. By May 2nd, they had joined Admiral Marc A. Mitscher's task force in the South Pacific. He was then involved in bombing attacks on various Japanese targets in the region. On September 2nd, 1944, they were assigned to join an attack on military targets on the island of Chichijima. Perhaps the best way to describe the attack is to quote George Bush's own words.

"The flak was the heaviest I'd ever flown into. The Japanese were ready and waiting: their anti-aircraft guns were set up to nail us as we pushed into our dives. By the time VT-51 was ready to go in, the sky was thick with angry black clouds of exploding anti-aircraft fire.

"Don Melvin led the way, scoring hits on a radio tower. I followed, going into a thirty-five degree dive, an angle of attack that sounds shallow, but in an Avenger felt as if you were headed straight down. The target map was strapped to my knee, and as I started into my dive, I'd already spotted the target area. Coming in, I was aware of black splotches of gunfire all around.

"Suddenly there was a jolt, as if a massive fist had crunched into the belly of the plane. Smoke poured into the cockpit, and I could see flames rippling across the crease of the wing, edging towards the fuel tanks. I stayed with the dive, homed in on the target, unloaded our four 500-pound bombs, and pulled away, heading for the sea. Once over water, I leveled off and told Delaney and White to bail out, turning the plane to starboard to take the slipstream off the door near Delaney's station.

"Up to that point, except for the sting of dense smoke blurring my vision, I was in fair shape. But when I went to make my jump, trouble came in pairs."

At a point approximately nine miles from the island of Minami-jima, Bush and one other person bailed out at about 3,000 feet. Bush's parachute opened and he landed safely in the sea, inflated his raft, and started paddling farther away from Chichijima. He was later picked up by the submarine USS *Finnback*.

Sadly, the other two members of Bush's Avenger crew failed to survive the attack; the parachute of the man seen to bail out failed to open.

Keep in mind that neither the turret gunner (Lt [jg] William White) nor the belly gunner/radioman (John Delaney) could wear their parachutes during operations in the Avenger. The man in the belly has to snap on his chest pack chute and crawl out the small door against a fierce air stream while the turret gunner drops down into the belly to follow suit. All this takes valuable time if the plane has been hit with anti-aircraft fire. It appears likely that the individual in the belly of Bush's TBM cleared the plane but not in time for his chute to open, while the turret gunner failed to clear the burning plane.

Sources: The George Bush Library and the Internet version of the Biography of George Herbert Walker Bush. *While permission to quote was requested of former President Bush on September 1st of 2003, no answer has been received to date.*

Bailout over India

Flying Officer C.V. Parker with No. 7 Sqn at Palam in New Delhi

"The 28th of October, 1952, was another bright day at the Indian Air Force air base at Hakimpet, where, as a newly graduated pilot, I was undergoing my applied phase of flying training on the last of the piston-engined fighter aircraft in the IAF-Spitfire and Tempest of World War II vintage. Navrose Lalkaka, my erstwhile flying instructor at the Air Force Academy (then at Begumpet), happened to be visiting, and listened quietly while Umesh Hosali, my instructor, briefed me for a routine practice sortie to be flown in Tempest II A, which at that moment was airborne on a similar training sortie flown by a co-pupil, Denny Satur.

"This was to be my thirteenth flight in this single-engined, single-seater fighter bomber, which quite dwarfed in size and performance the tiny little fabric-covered Tiger Moth trainer aircraft, and the ubiquitous Harvard trainer aircraft that together represented the (then) sum total of my 180 hours of flying experience during the basic and advanced phases of flying training those days.

"Denny taxied the Tempest onto the changeover dispersal, gave me the 'thumbs up' sign to indicate that the aircraft was fully serviceable, and, while the engines kept running, helped me to strap into the aircraft. Conscious of the fact that my old instructor was watching me from Flying Control, I taxied out carefully, lined up on the runway, made a final check of instruments, and took off (as straight as I could) to climb into our local flying area.

"Fifteen minutes later and 3,000 feet up in the air, without any warning my (hitherto) safe world exploded dangerously. The engine had caught fire, its covering panels bursting open right in front of my disbelieving eyes, and smoke and flames engulfed me inside the cockpit. Gasping for air and almost blinded, I managed to transmit a hasty and feeble 'May Day' call on the radio to indicate a grave emergency, while simultaneously trying to undo my straps, disconnect myself from the various attachments to the aircraft, and jettison the canopy to bail out of the aircraft, which was now rapidly losing height and getting out of my control.

"After two desperate but unsuccessful attempts, I finally succeeded in inverting the aircraft and dropping out. After the mandatory (but I suspect rather hurried) count to ten, I pulled the rip cord to deploy the emergency parachute, which opened and jerked me into an upright position.

"Suddenly I found myself drifting gently earthwards under the canopy of a parachute for the first time in my life while the Tempest exploded in mid-air somewhere just below me. I glanced down at the brown earth below (closing in a bit too rapidly for comfort!), and was aghast to discover that I was in my socks—my shoes having been 'sucked off' somewhere during the bail-out. (This was prior to the introduction of flying boots as mandatory equipment for aircrew.) I tried to recollect all the lessons we had been given on how to 'touch down' in a parachute, but none had covered 'landing' in bare feet! Unknown to me at that moment forty-three years ago, I had just become eligible for membership in the world's most exclusive organization, the Caterpillar Club."

This narrative comes from the memoirs of Air Vice Marshal Cecil Vivian Parker, MVC, VM, on the Internet, and with written permisssion.

Bailing out over Belgium, 1944

Mike Ciano's Date for Joining the Caterpillar Club

M ike's story is not very different from many stories of escapes from four-engine bombers, many of which have been recorded—some in this book. What is different is that it records an escape where every member of the crew escaped alive, and this was a rarity during World War II. Too many flyers were killed during the attacks, by parachutes that didn't open properly, by angry citizens on the ground, or by drowning in the sea.

"With improved weather on the early morning of April 12th, 1944, the 8th Air Force sent the heavy bombers to the Schweinfurt area. I was the tail gunner on Joe Pavelka's crew with the 445th Bomb Group, a part of the 2nd Air Division that was headed to Zwickau, Germany.

"As our trip to Zwickau progressed, I remember dense clouds filled the sky. Our B-24 bombers were producing heavy contrails. This gave an advantage to the enemy fighters hiding in our contrails firing rockets at us. Just before reaching the German border, orders were issued to return to base, aborting the mission because of the deteriorating weather in Germany.

"Soon after turning back into Belgium, our navigator Lt. Phil Solomon's voice was heard on the intercom informing everyone that bandits were attacking at one o'clock high.

"Flak hit the far left engine, and black smoke started pouring out of it. A hole about the size of a basketball was opened up at the feet of S/Sgt. Wayne Luce, the waist gunner. S/Sgt. Pete Clark unzipped the windbreaker in the tail and yelled to me, 'We have to throw out S/Sgt. Luce. He has been hit badly in several places.'

"Suddenly another direct hit just ahead of where I was standing, ripping open the floor. S/Sgt. Clark and I lifted Luce up to the waist window and as we pushed him out, I pulled the 'rip cord.' Fortunately, the chute opened and with that we both looked at each other and smiled.

"The enemy attackers looked like a swarm of bees heading for our formation. Lt. Phil Solomon saw about twenty to forty enemy FW–190s lining up to attack our group, flying two at a time with their 20mm cannons firing into the formations of B–24 bombers. Someone on the intercom screamed out, 'We've been hit!' as the 20mm shells began popping inside the plane, starting a fire. The natural reaction to fire in a bomber is to evacuate the plane without delay. The radio operator, Sgt. Richard Hanson, grabbed his chute and started for the nearest exit. In the meantime Sgt. Chester Hincewicz left his position in the top turret and brought a fire extinguisher to the radio room. Here he found panic among the gunners. He caught Richard before he jumped and they both began trying to put out the fire. Their efforts were in vain. Everyone resumed his gun position when word came over the intercom that the nose of the ship was hit and the bombardier was wounded.

"A few minutes later, bullets were ricocheting in the tail turret, and just as quickly I spotted a Me109 coming toward us at eye level. As soon as I thought he was in hitting range, I opened up, and in seconds saw a ball of fire coming from the Me109, and I was not quite sure what it was. By now our ship was bouncing and losing altitude, so we were forced to leave the formation from our 'Tail-End Charley' position.

"We were now on our own like a sitting duck getting hit on all sides. The plane vibrated as we fired our guns in an attempt to keep the enemy fighters from attacking.

"With our intercom shot out, S/Sgt. Chet Hincewicz came to the tail to tell Pete Clark and me to get ready to bail out. I quickly got out of the tail turret and when I looked out the left waist window I saw fire coming out of the far left engine. The fuselage was now filled with smoke. I suddenly realized the chips were down and I was about to do what no gunner ever dreamed of doing—bailing out.

"We moved about inside the plane like we were in a fog. While all this mess was taking place, I suddenly realized I didn't have my chute and I quickly moved to the tail to get it. I was stricken with panic when I saw it starting to catch fire. I quickly put it out and hooked it on my parachute harness. Luckily, just the outer cords got singed. Gunners never had their chutes on because they felt hampered.

"Exhausted and off oxygen at 22,000 feet, we decided to jump out the camera hatch instead of getting up and out the waist window. As I was sitting with my legs hanging out and getting enough nerve to drop out, I suddenly heard a piercing sound and a sting across my forehead. Before I had the time to investigate Sgt. Clark tapped me on the shoulder to drop down and out. I gave a last look down and before I had the time to clear the ship, I pulled the cord.

"Looking up, I saw the ship moving away and wondered what lay ahead at the moment. When I hit the sky I experienced a sensation that can only be describe as 'unreal,' because I was in a half daze, 'out of touch,' because for the first time I experienced the feeling of being very much alone. I could only describe it as 'beautiful and scary,' because of the absolute stillness and weird feeling of being motionless, never to come down. Naturally all of this faded away when I passed through the clouds. I quickly realized I was falling, but the feeling was not apparent until I was eye level with trees and buildings. Before I could blink my eyes, I felt the ground quickly rushing up at me. As soon as I hit the cobblestoned street, a stinging pain ran from my ankles up to my head and I buckled up and passed out.

"When I opened my eyes I saw German soldiers looking down at me, mumbling. I looked beyond and saw people gawking at me. I was then carried to what looked like an American-type police wagon and driven to a school hall.

"I was there overnight and then put on a bus that carried four of my crewmembers. They were the bombardier, Lt. William T. Burtt, ball turret gunner, S/Sgt. Robert T. Hansen, waist gunner S/Sgt. Wade R. Luce, and radio operator, Richard Hanson.

"The guards kept us apart and silent. I couldn't find out a thing. They all appeared okay to me, but somewhat scared.

"Sometime later I arrived at the walled-in hospital in Brussels where I was carried in. This was the last time I saw my bombardier, Lt. Burtt. S/Sgt. Hansen and I met up again at *DuLag Luft*, the interrogating center just outside of Frankfurt, Germany. I remained in the hospital occupied solely by wounded German *Luftwaffe* personnel. Every morning a '*Luftwaffe*' colonel doctor would enter the ward and a German nurse just ahead of him would shout, '*Achtung!*'

"April 18th came around, but because of the circumstances I did not have a party to celebrate my twenty-third birthday. This didn't prevent the guards from celebrating Hitler's birthday on the 20th. The champagne was plentiful, because the guards were going back for refills over and over again. Had Hitler's parents been able to look into the future, they would have changed their minds and kept the bedroom light on.

"After a week of recuperating from my wounds, I was allowed to go out into the walled courtyard. I sat in the sun and watched our bombers and fighters fly over. It was somewhat of an odd feeling to look up and realize they are free in enemy skies and you're a captive. It somehow didn't seem real in the least. Many times I would wait anxiously for their return and take note of the formation pattern to see if they had a rough mission. It was also very depressing to me when watching them head northwesterly as free as 'birds' back to England. For me, well, I was just scared and wondered what the hell was in store. It was just a question of time when I would be sent to Germany and who knew what.

"Here is what happened to my crewmembers (from my post-war research):

Joe Pavelka, Pilot, evaded to Switzerland
Albert P. Gilsdorf, Copilot, POW
Philip Solomon, Navigator, evaded to Switzerland
William T. Burtt, Bombardier, POW
Chester B. Hincewicz, Engineer, evaded in Belgium
Richard F. Hanson , Radio Opr., POW, *Stalag Luft* IV
Wade R. Luce, Ball Turret, POW
Robert T. Hansen, Waist Gunner, POW, *Stalag Luft* IV
Peter M. Clark, Waist Gunner, evaded, France
Michael R. Ciano, Tail Gunner, POW."

From personal communication by Michael R. Ciano.

"Lucky Lindy," the Ace of caterpillars

How Charles Lindbergh Set a Record in the Four Jumps He Made

Everybody, especially those involved in aviation industry, knows the story of Charles Augustus Lindbergh and his history-making flight in 1927 to Le Bourget Airport in Paris, France. This was the first solo flight to be made from North America to Europe across the wide Atlantic Ocean.

Perhaps less well known are those days between Lindbergh's first sight of an airplane in 1912, and the day he decided to make the transatlantic flight. These fifteen years were spent mostly in achieving one sure goal: to fly a plane. There were many bends and curves and other impediments in his way before he finally achieved that flying "licence" (although that was only a word in those early days). Finally, in 1924, he joined the U.S. Army for flight training and received his silver wings in June of the following year.

Charles didn't even wait to get those wings before he made his first emergency jump. On March 5th, 1925, at 5,000 feet and in a single-seated SE-5 scout biplane, he and another cadet collided as they went in to attack an "enemy" DH4B bomber. After he closed the throttle and checked that the other pilot, Lt. McCallister, was unhurt, he removed his belt, climbed out onto the trailing edge of the wing, and jumped out backwards, as far as possible from the plane.

With the wreckage falling almost straight down, and with his fear that it may well fall on him, Charles put off pulling the rip cord until he had dropped several hundred feet and into the clouds. The parachute opened perfectly, and the next thing he did was to search for a suitable landing place. He was over mesquite and drifting towards a ploughed field, which he was almost able to reach by "slipping" the chute. He landed on the side of a ditch less than 100 feet from the mesquite, tumbling, although he was not injured. The canopy was kept open by the wind and would not collapse until Charles had pulled on one set of shroud lines to let the air out.

Lindbergh's second jump came on June 2nd, 1925, after he had received his pilot's wings. He was chief pilot for the Robertson Aircraft Corporation of St. Louis, Missouri, a company that made commercial planes. During a test flight, he was doing spins when the plane he was in failed to respond to his attempts to recover. Instead, the plane plummeted earthward, twisting and turning. It was said by observers that Charles and the plane parted company at 250 feet, although Charles insists it was higher, at 350 feet.

His parachute opened immediately after he passed by the stabilizer and then it was a matter of staying out of the way of the falling plane. Passing less than twenty-five feet from his parachute, the plane crashed into a grain field. A high wind was pushing Charles towards some high-tension poles, so he partially deflated the canopy to hasten descent and avoid the wires. He landed solidly in a potato patch, then was dragged several feet across a road by the wind before several men were able to collapse the chute for him.

Charles suffered a dislocated shoulder in the drop, but was back flying again within two hours.

The third jump came a few months later while Charles was involved in flying the mail. On September 16th, 1926, as he was trying to complete a long flight at night in blinding snow and rain, his plane ran out of fuel. At 5,000 feet, the engine sputtered and died. Lindbergh climbed up onto the cowling and jumped out over the right side of the cockpit, pulling the rip cord after about 100 feet of fall. The risers pulled him into an upright position, which he hoped would see him to the ground below.

However, the plane, which had almost stopped dead when he jumped, started up again as it nosed down, and additional unknown fuel was fed to the engine. The plunging plane spiralled around Charles at least five times, each time a little farther away, before crashing about two miles away from where Charles came down. The mail was undamaged and was later delivered by train.

The fourth, and thankfully the last, of Lindbergh's jumps took place just shortly after his third. It was November 3rd, 1926. Again it was while carrying the mail, and again it was during inclement weather when the fuel tanks were running dry. Rather than attempt to land blindly, he dove over the side of the cockpit while at 13,000 feet and moving at seventy mph. When Charles pulled the rip cord, the parachute opened perfectly, and soon he was heading for the ground.

But this time it was not his plane that created problems; it was oscillations of the parachute. For over five minutes, it kept swinging him, until he neared the ground when the snow turned to rain and the oscillations slowed. Then Lindbergh landed on a barbed-wire fence, but thankfully his heavy flying suit prevented any injury from the barbs. The wind kept the canopy inflated again and it took several minutes before he was able to deflate it.

But, as the saying goes, the mail will get through, and again it did—even if slightly oil-soaked.

I don't think all these jumps, and the practice they provided, would have helped Lindbergh one whit during his long flight to Le Bourget. However, they certainly would have if he had been able to partake in wartime flying, as many other Caterpillars did.

Adapted from Charles Lindbergh, an American Aviator, *with the permission of the author, James Bates.*

the accidental exit

How F/L Bob Brinkhurst Found Himself in a Parachute, and Nobody Shot at Him

flight Lieutenant D.J. Cox was an instructor at Bassingbourne in England, and on July 9th, 1963, flew with Flight Lieutenant Brinkhurst of the RCAF on a standardization exercise. As a result of a servicing error, Brinkhurst was ejected. What happened can perhaps best be told in the words of the pilots themselves.

The Instructor's Story

"It was July 9th, I don't need to refer to my log book; this date I remember! I was flying with Bob Brinkhurst on a standardization exercise, an exercise concerned with the asymmetrical problems of the Canberra. I had just demonstrated how to find the minimum safe control speed on one engine at full power, with the undercarriage down, and then it was Bob's turn. He is a big, strong chap, no difficulty in reaching and holding full rudder, so I just sat back to watch. It was going well, the Canberra, slightly nose up, was climbing slowly. Bob had full rudder on and was gently applying bank towards the live engine; my attention was divided between looking out and [checking] the airspeed, my feet resting lightly on the rudder pedals, my hands in my lap. The speed was approximately 135 knots, height 1,800 feet, when the aircraft started to yaw very slightly.

"'That's it, Bob,' I thought, 'time to recover.' but I didn't get round to telling him.

"The noise of the explosion was terrific; it left my ears ringing. The cockpit, briefly, was full of acrid smoke. I felt a sharp pain in my right elbow and my left foot catapulted back towards me.

"'****!! We've been hit,' I thought, 'we'll have to get out!'

"It seemed a long time before I realized that Bob wasn't there any more, just a gaping space on my right, no canopy over my head. I turned to reassure Sgt. Brian Webb, the navigator, that the plane was still airworthy, and there was no need for him to consider abandoning ship."

The Student Instructor's Story

"I was flying in the right-hand seat of a Mk T.4 Canberra at approximately 1,800 feet during an asymmetric training exercise. As I attained minimum control speed of approximately 135 knots, my ejection seat fired unexpectedly. The noise of the ejection and subsequent wind blast, and the sudden acceleration, momentarily confused me. When I realized that I was clear of the aircraft and descending, the seat harness had already automatically released me and I seemed to be in a flat spin facing upwards. The seat was at my left side, attached to me in some unknown manner, which convinced me that the parachute was not going to open automatically.

"I immediately pulled the outer 'D' ring and, although I could not reach the manual override handle, I pulled the inner 'D' ring, hoping that the parachute would still open. Shortly afterwards, I felt a slight tug as the parachute opened.

"Almost immediately, it seemed, I struck the ground with a severe jolt. There had been insufficient time to orientate myself before landing, and I had no recollection of seeing the ground until a split second before I landed."

Eyewitnesses on the ground stated that the parachute opened at 100 feet; even a second's delay would have proved fatal. Fortunately Brinkhurst's injuries were minor.

The cause of the accidental ejection was proved by the enquiry board to be mechanical error. However, the cool heads that prevailed, both in the plane and in the parachute, saved at least one life. Even the instructor who was left behind reacted quickly to dissuade the navigator, third man in the plane, from following Bob Brinkhurst out.

Details taken from the RAF Bomber Command Review, *October 1963, and from personal communication with Flight Lieutenant Bob Brinkhurst.*

"Ready if you need us . . ."

free fall over shiphdam

Forrest S. Clark's Emergency Bailout in 1943

Sgt. Forrest Clark's moment of truth came close to suddenly happening over the North Sea, while returning from a bombing raid on the continent. As a tail gunner on a B-24 of the 44th Bomb Group, the U.S. 8th Air Force, his formation was attacked by wave after wave of German twin-engine fighters. During the attacks, Sgt. Clark was successful in shooting down one of them.

The German planes attacked from all sides, firing 20-millimetre shells through his rear turret just above his head. Then they zoomed under the B-24 and up the sides, where the waist gunners could get their shots in. Clark kept firing until he was almost out of ammunition. One of the waist gunners was bringing more ammunition for the rear turret when he was hit in the head by a 20-mm shell, and rendered unconscious and bleeding.

Clark heard the bailout bell suddenly sound, but he had difficulty getting out of his shattered tail turret. Behind him he saw two men getting ready to jump through the open camera hatch in the floor of the plane. Finally out of his turret, he prayed, because he knew he would not survive long in the ice-cold sea if he jumped.

"I actually went down on my knees and prayed. There I was, looking down at the frigid North Sea from 12,000 feet with a parachute I wasn't sure how to use. I didn't know anything about parachutes or jumping; that was not part of our training.

"Fortunately, just about that time the fighter attacks stopped, and the Germans left us to what they must have thought would be our deaths. So, we ignored the bailout bell. Nobody wanted to leave the wounded gunner behind."

The pilot, Lt. R.C. Griffith, told the crew that their plane was in serious trouble; only one engine was good, and the other three were faltering badly. Along with another badly damaged B-24, they sputtered along towards the British coast, losing altitude all the time. The other B-24 finally crash-landed on the North Sea, fifty miles short of the English coast. Clark's plane circled the spot while sending out requests for rescue. Then they sputtered on.

More than once the pilot told the crew to prepare to ditch, but the wounded gunner would surely die if they landed in the icy water. So, with all the engines threatening to quit, and the plane stuttering as if in its death throes, they limped on until the English coast slid beneath the bomber.

But they were not yet home free! The landing gear refused to work, so trying to land the plane would be hazardous to all aboard. So the bailout bell clamoured again, and the pilot ordered everybody out; he would stay with the wounded gunner.

Clark squatted over the rear camera hatch, closed his eyes, and jumped. Then he felt himself falling through space, but with his eyes still closed. He counted slowly to ten, which was what they were told to do. This would get them well away from the plane and avoid getting tangled with the stabilizers or tail assembly. Then Clark counted to ten twice more to increase the safety factor. When he finally opened his eyes, Clark saw the earth coming up in a hurry, so he pulled the rip cord in a hurry. He landed bang in the middle of a plowed field.

Just as he was ready to land, Clark saw the farmer running across the field, pitchfork in hand and menacing look on his face.

Clark's first thought was that they had made a navigation error, and this was occupied Holland. But when the farmer told him he was back in England, he wanted to get down and kiss the ground.

The pilot managed to land the plane on one wheel and save the life of the wounded gunner. When the wreckage was later checked, two unexploded shells were found in the one good engine that had helped bring this crew safely home.

Maybe Somebody heard Sgt. Clark's prayers.

This story is reproduced with permission from Parachutes, Yesterday/ Today/ Tomorrow, *owned and published by James M. Bates of Windsor Locks, Connecticut, USA.*

other faces, other chutes

In any vast treasure trove of stories, from which the foregoing have been drawn, there is often the problem of which ones to pick. Even if we printed only two pages from each of the of the 100,000 stories, our product would probably outdo the Encyclopedia Britannica in sheer volume. And who, in all his or her lifetime, would be able to, or want to, read it?

With the aim of maintaining an interest in the subject of "Caterpillars," I have kept the number of stories to what I consider a reasonable number of interesting ones. I trust that the readers will agree with me.

However, there are some stories that deserve mention, not because of their length, but due to their uniqueness—something that happened during the bailout that made them different from the norm. That is the purpose of this chapter: to say a few words about the unusual.

One of them is about F/L Joe Herman, a pilot with the RAAF and serving on 466 Squadron in RAF Bomber Command. The night of November 4th, 1944, on his 32nd operation, Joe took his plane and crew to Bockhum in the Ruhr. Right after bombing, Joe's plane was hit by anti-aircraft fire and set aflame. Escape was the order of the day.

Two members of the crew managed to bail out of the plane before it exploded, but Joe was blown out of the plane when this happened (the other four crew members died in the explosion). However, Joe had not had a chance to clip on his parachute pack, and was falling without one. This is not recommended if one wishes a soft landing.

Falling through space, screaming, "Oh God, don't let me die like this!" suddenly Joe hit something solid. He heard a voice say, "Is there anybody around?" It was the voice of Irish Vivash, the mid-upper gunner, who had successfully bailed out, but with a badly wounded leg. Grasping Irish's good leg, Joe held on until the two of them landed heavily, but safely.

Another "free fall" was by Alan Magee, a gunner on a B–17 with the 303rd Bomb Group of the U.S. 8th Air Force. They were on a mission to St. Nazaire, France, in January of 1943, when his bomber was set aflame by enemy gunfire. Alan was thrown from the plane before even having a chance to buckle on his parachute. He fell 20,000 feet and crashed through the skylight of the St. Nazaire train station. His arm was badly injured, but he recovered from this and other injuries.

One of the first Lady Caterpillars was reported to be Fay Gillis Wells, one of the Charter Members and a co-founder of the famous Ninety-Nines, an organization of women flyers. She was flying in a plane with her instructor, upside down over Long Island, and when the plane flew apart, Fay was thrown out. It took her several minutes to find the rip cord, but the parachute did open at 400 feet. So, Ms Wells bailed out on September 1st, 1929, although there are some rumors that an Irene McFarlane preceded her by four years.

Bill Brinn, an air gunner on a B–26 Marauder, bailed out over Angers in France on August 1st, 1944. His story is a little more "painful" than many of the others, but he is one of the few who saw the pain in place before the enemy action had occurred.

Bill had a gigantic boil on his rear end, and located just where the parachute harness was to have been secured. So he flew the mission without all of the harness in place. During the escape, Bill was sitting on the edge of the escape hatch, when suddenly the aircraft spun in and started heading earthward. He was thrown clear.

Falling towards earth, Bill worked desperately to secure the straps. With the ground getting closer, he barely managed to get this done and open his chute. This close shave seemed to strike Bill as rather funny. However, less funny was the fact that, shortly after his landing, the boil broke, and then the real pain started.

Perhaps a somewhat more typical bailout was done by Stan Jolly of Australia when he had to "hit the silk." Just after leaving the target, Mailly-le-Camp in northern France, the bullets started hitting the metal. The pilot immediately told the crew to bail out. Jolly disconnected his oxygen and intercom, clipped on his parachute (not realizing that the D-ring was on the right side, while he was left-handed), and walked to the escape hatch.

Lifting the hatch door out of the floor, and turning it diagonally, he threw it out. However, the slipstream caught it and jammed the door back into the opening. With the small resulting escape area, Jolly had to squeeze himself out until he was just hanging by his fingertips. Letting go, he let out a yell (somehow thinking he was on a roller coaster) and was clear of the aircraft. After a brief floating sensation, Jolly pulled the rip cord (but could not recall which hand he used). Floating down, he watched his plane become just a ball of fire in the night sky. Jolly eventually landed heavily in a plowed field, beside a forest. Hiding his parachute and harness, he set off in an easterly direction for safety.

However, if Jolly's bailout was considered "more typical," then I am certainly glad mine was much less than that.

One of the most notable bailouts was that of Group Captain Sir Douglas Bader, the well-known "legless" ace of the RAF. Sir Douglas had lost both legs in a flying accident prior to the war, but had been able to convince the air force to put him back into flying status once he was equipped with metal legs. In August of 1942, as commanding officer of 242 Squadron, he had just led a swoop over Northern France when he collided with a German BF-109 fighter plane.

Forced to bail out, Sir Douglas was also forced to leave one of his false legs behind in the cockpit, as it had jammed on him. He was captured on landing, and his captors sent out a notice to the RAF that they could drop a replacement leg, unmolested, into *Stalag Luft* III, where he was then a prisoner. The RAF demurred, feeling this was privileged treatment, but dropped a replacement leg anyway, under full combat conditions.

A few other bailouts of note include the following: Lt. Col. I.M. Chissov, of the Russian Air Force, fell 23,000 feet without a parachute and survived, though badly injured. Unfortunately, Russian records are not available, so we can't describe this fall.

Captain Joseph Kittinger, of the U.S. Air Force, fell 102,200 feet from the gondola on a balloon over New Mexico. He fell free for four minutes and thirty-eight seconds through 84,700 feet before opening his parachute system, reaching a peak speed of 629 mph. While not a "Caterpillar" jump, it is indicative of the heights achieved. (His parachute system had to include an airtight, high-altitude costume with oxygen, or he would not have survived those high altitudes.)

The first recorded jump to escape occurred on March 1st, 1912, over St. Louis, Missouri, by Captain Albert Berry from 1,640 feet.

However, to surpass in time all of our Caterpillars or other jumpers, we have to go back almost two centuries to find the very first life saving by parachute. On July 14th, 1808, Jordaki Kuparento, a Polish balloonist, entered the history books as the first person to save his life by using a parachute. Rising over Warsaw in a "fire balloon," flames from his portable heat source in the balloon's passenger basket (fuel was said to be bundles of straw lighted as needed) flared upward, reached the balloon fabric, and burned rapidly. The balloon lost its form, and Kuparento started his fall to earth. However, the balloonist had had foresight, and quickly equipped himself with a parachute that he had wisely brought along.

His lifesaving apparatus was reported to be a foldable silk parachute that he had made himself, one with handgrips formed at the end of suspension lines. Firmly clutching his folded canopy, he launched himself and his parachute bundle from the basket. The canopy snapped open sharply, almost causing Kuparento to lose his tight grip. But he hung on desperately and landed safely on the ground.

These stories are but a drop in the bucket against all those aviators who have been forced to strap on, use the escape hatch, and pull the rip cord to save their lives since aviation was developed (with apologies to Dolly Shepherd and Louie May and, of course, Jordaki Kuparento). It would be very good if every story were written up, but of course this would be impossible in light of our limited lifetime. Perhaps if God is good to the author and grants him another twenty years or more, Volume II might come of it.

But for the moment if these thirty-some bailout stories create some pleasure for the reader, and perhaps some caution if the reader is ever forced to strap on a parachute, then I am pleased.

However, unmentioned so far in the stories is the one rigid rule by which all Caterpillars must abide: When escaping from an airplane, and using the parachute to effect this escape, it is expected that the escaper would retain possession of the D-ring. This should then be returned to the person who originally packed the chute.

Failure to comply with this rule would, under normal circumstances, result in the debt, by the escaper, of one large bottle of good Scotch whisky to the appropriate packer. With some 100,000 members of the Caterpillar Club, and the complete lack of any record of fulfillment of this debt, we do have the resources for the establishment of a small distillery in the highlands of Scotland.

As the self-appointed surrogate for all of the past and present deprived parachute packers, the author is willing to accept donations towards the establishment of this distillery.

As a final note, I must refer to that anonymous New Zealand airman who bailed out and landed safely by way of an Irvin parachute: he wrote to Leslie Irvin those immortal words that supplied our title, "Bless You, Brother Irvin!"

All of these stories were received by communications from the Caterpillar involved and from the Internet; that of Jordaki Kuparento was by the kind permission of James Bates.

the Locals

This is for all those Caterpillars who live near me, and say, "Hey, where's our stories?"

As a member of the RCAF Ex-Prisoners of War Association (on sufferance only) and the current secretary-treasurer, I am surrounded mainly by guys who were also Caterpillars. They bailed out just before becoming prisoners. I tell them, time after time, that I am writing a book on their use of the parachute, but it is only when they see the finished product almost ready that the requests for inclusion begin to come in!

So, in order to be able to attend future meetings with as free a conscience as possible, I am dedicating this section to those guys whom I see almost every day. As Jesus said to Peter, during the Last Supper, "You will deny me three times!" Well, I am not going to give these guys that opportunity any more.

The first of the locals is **Ian Fowler**, or rather, Flying Officer Fowler. Ian was with the RCAF and trained as a navigator/radar operator. His pilot was an Australian, Pilot Officer Desmond Snape, and the two of them flew Mosquito Night Fighters on 141 Squadron, of 100 Group. Equipped with the most modern of homing equipment, they flew over Europe to provide support to the Allied bomber force.

On the night of February 24th, 1944, Mosquito #943 was patrolling the Kiel-Kattigat region, to protect aircraft in the area, when Ian picked up an enemy radar contact. The pilot went to full power to begin an attack on the enemy aircraft. Just as they were closing, the starboard engine overheated and blew up, losing all of its coolant. Coupled with an exchange of gunfire, the damaged Mosquito was forced to break off and dive for cover. After an hour, and losing altitude all the time, it became obvious they were not going to make it back to England.

So, with the options of landing on the ice-cold North Sea, or bailing out over land, the pilot sent out a "Mayday" call and said to abandon ship. The escape door was at Ian's feet, and, though they had practised it many a time at base, it did not open easily at this most critical time. With supreme effort, Ian finally kicked it free and tumbled out into the black night. A few minutes after pulling the D-ring, he touched down, but suffered a sprained ankle from the speed of the fall.

Ian lay there until first light, when he hid his parachute and headed for an isolated Dutch farm. The family Kuipers welcomed him into their home; but on his way, someone had spotted him and reported this to the local German commandant. Shortly after, Ian was arrested by the soldiers and his remaining war days were spent in *Stalag Luft* III.

A few days after the landing, Ian was taken to see the dead body of his pilot, P/O Snape, who had not been able to escape the plane. If the escape door had operated properly, both flyers would be alive today.

Post-war, Ian worked as an engineer with Esso Petroleum in Calgary, and enjoyed a successful career with them in many parts of the world. Today he is retired, and lives with his wife Dorothy in Calgary.

The next story is that of **Doug Hawkes**, a pilot with the #419 "Moose" Squadron. Doug was also with the RCAF. Based at Middleton-St-George in Durham, and on his fifth operation, he and his crew were assigned to be part of a raid on Magdeburg for the night of January 21st, 1944, flying one of the Halifax II's with which the squadron was equipped.

With a replacement rear gunner, F/S Wilf Barnes (who was on his twenty-eighth trip and had two kills to his credit), they set out. Over the North Sea, WO2 Don McDevitt, the wireless operator, reported their radio to be unserviceable. But they flew on and, after circuiting the target once, dropped their bombs. Then they headed for home.

"How much further to enemy shores?" asked Hawkes, the pilot.

"Two minutes," was the immediate reply from F/S John Fletcher, the navigator, and these were the last words he ever spoke.

Suddenly the plane was hit in the port wing by predicted flak. Both engines were knocked out, and John Fletcher was killed. The bomb aimer, Frank Houison, was slightly wounded, and Hawkes was hit in the upper right arm, making it difficult for him to handle the controls. The flight engineer, Sgt. Don Board of the RAF, helped him to regain level flight, and in a southeasterly direction so they would be over land if it became necessary to jump. Ditching in the North Sea, in mid-January, was not an option they wanted to take. When it was obvious they could not return to England, Flight Sergeant Hawkes ordered, "Abandon Aircraft." Six out of the seven crewmembers were successful in reaching the ground by parachute. In Hawkes's own words,

"I had difficulty pulling the parachute release pin with my right arm, but eventually succeeded with my left. It did not seem long before I neared the ground and I was able to do it in a downwind direction. We had had plenty of practice on the procedures and it usually worked just fine. I spilled the wind out of my canopy as I came to rest in a cold, muddy, farmer's field. With broken harness equipment, it took almost half an hour to get free of it. I hid it all and then walked until I found an open door in a U-shaped farm building; entered, climbed into a loft, and tried to sleep. Shortly I spotted what I thought was a Dutchman, but who turned out to be a loyal German farmer. That was the end of my freedom."

The trip by Douglas Hawkes and his crew was on the same night and the same target as my first, and we may have seen his plane go down, just as our plane was turning west to cross the

BLESS YOU, *Brother Irvin*

North Sea for home. We were riddled by flak, but fortunately not badly enough to share the fate of Doug Hawkes and his crew.

After the war, Douglas spent a successful career in the real estate industry of Calgary. He is now retired, and lives with his wife Dorothy in the suburb of Douglasdale.

Jack Kupsick is my brother-in-law, but he was also my roommate many years ago. The two of us were evaders hiding out with the French Resistance until the Allied armies reached our section and liberated us. How he became my brother-in-law is another story, but how he became an evader is even more interesting.

Jack was a navigator on a Boeing B-17 and on February 8th, 1944, was on the way to Frankfurt, Germany. With the adverse weather conditions, the German fighters attacked early while the bomber force was still on the way to the target. "Tail-End Charlies," of which Jack's plane was one, received special attention with head-on attacks. His bombardier was killed, and Jack himself was wounded in his hand and arm. The plane caught fire in the bomb bay and a wing.

The order to bail out soon came. Jack had been blessed with a combination of an American harness and a British chest pack that would only fit on the harness one way, with the D-ring handle on his left side. With that arm having been hit by a 20mm cannon round, he had to jam his wounded hand into the D-ring (rip cord) before he jumped. After diving head first out of the forward escape hatch, the weight of his hand and arm popped the parachute almost immediately, while they were at high altitude.

Fortunately he fell through several layers of clouds, so he was not pursued or shot at while he descended—which was happening to others at the time. He did have some anxious moments, however, as his chute collapsed six times on the way down. Suffice it to say that he was relieved that it reopened each time, and stayed open until he touched down, which was as easy as stepping off a chair.

A civilian ran up and helped him unbuckle, since his wounded arm and hand were not cooperating. He had lost his right flying boot, with the heated shoe inside it, during the descent, so they put his left flying boot onto his right foot, and Jack took off running with two left feet. The civilian took off in the opposite direction with his "silk umbrella to safety." He lost the D-ring and never collected a Caterpillar; but a parachute had saved his life, which led to freedom via the French Underground. During the final three months of his stay with them, he was quartered on a farm with the author and his navigator.

For many years after the war, the author searched, unsuccessfully, for Jack, but was unable to find him. In May of 1991, at a reunion of evaders in Anaheim, California, there he was! Unbeknownst to the author, Jack had decided to stay in the military, and had completed his term of enlistment through both the Korean and Vietnam wars. Apparently one bailout was not enough for this airman!

Many years later, I introduced Jack to my sister Shirley, and now we are brothers-in-law.

**"Caterpillars All!" L–R: Bob Lindsay, Virgil Marco,
John Harms, John Kupsick, John Neal.**

Willie was the mid-upper gunner on a Lancaster in #103 Squadron, and on December 13th, 1944, was on the way home from Essen on his ninth trip. What follows is a story of raw courage and ultimate sacrifice.

"We had dropped steadily from our bombing altitude of around 17,000 feet, when we felt the sudden jolt. The skipper came over the intercom: "What's that?" I looked out of my turret and saw a five-inch hole in the right wing, petrol pouring out of it. I reported this to the skipper and he feathered the engine nearest to where the hole was. However, almost at once flames broke out and the plane was on fire.

"'Abandon Aircraft! Abandon Aircraft!' was the last call sent out over the intercom. I sat frozen for a few seconds; not with fear, but thinking, 'This can't be happening—not to us! Where's my chute?' and 'Which door would be best?' Then climbing down from my turret in the darkness, the plane started to bounce and twist around something awful. I found my chute where I had stored it and headed to the rear escape door; but the handle of the door was missing.

"Rather than waste time looking for the handle, I headed for the front escape hatch. Not a soul was in sight and everything I touched along the fuselage was hot. When I finally reached the cockpit, there was Eddy, our rear gunner, talking to the pilot. But Eddy did not have a parachute on. He was my best pal, only nineteen years old, and we were the only Canadians in the crew. When I asked him where his chute was, his answer was to fling out his arms indicating it had opened in the plane. It was no longer of any use in a jump situation.

"Having learned how to handle a wounded man on one parachute, I pleaded with Eddy to jump with me, using just my parachute. All he would say was 'No, No! The skipper is going to land the plane O.K.' No matter how much I begged, he refused to come with me. I asked the skipper what I should do, and he said, 'We're down to 5,000 feet now. Jump, Willie! That's an order! Jump!'

"I stepped to the front of the plane and into the nose, looking back. There was my pal Eddie and the skipper. For a second or two I froze. I thought to myself, 'I can't leave them; what can I do?' Then the skipper's words, 'That's an order' went through my mind.

"I fell through the opening and into the cold night. I don't remember pulling the rip cord but I must have as I had the D-ring in my hands. So I dropped it. Then I saw the flaming airplane spiraling down and burning in the distance. I knew right then that Eddie and the skipper had perished.

"I must have tied my harness on very loosely, as it seems I could have fallen out of it on either side. I still had on both flying boots, as they were fastened to my electric suit. I began to smell the land as I got lower, and with a jerk, I was hung up on the branch of a tree. Then I fell again, this time onto the ground below. Feeling around, I found nothing broken.

"So that I would not be found by the Germans, I dragged my parachute, through the rain and mud, over to a large toppled tree that was lying nearby. Crawling underneath this tree, I wrapped myself up in the parachute to wait out the search. I stayed there for a day, listening to the searchers looking, unsuccessfully, for me. Then the next evening, with the search over, I moved on and was for the following ten days on the loose before I was captured.

"I still look back, and grieve, that I had to leave my pals, but I've never been able to change what happened. However, I do proudly wear my ruby-eyed Caterpillar, for without it these past sixty years would not have been. Thank you, Leslie Irvin!"

At the request of this Caterpillar, I have not used his real name. The memories of his jump, and the following deaths of his friends, are still too vivid, even after fifty-nine years. After the war, Willie spent a successful career in the construction industry and built many houses that now are part of Calgary. On May 7th, 2004, Willie died at Rosedale Hospice, ending a long life of service to his fellow prisoners of war and others.

Frank Robert Anton was an air observer with the Royal Air Force, and he and his crew might have been members of the famous Pathfinder Force had it not been for some very accurate anti-aircraft fire over Nürnberg. The raid was in February of 1943, and just as they were releasing their 1,000-pound bomb and their incendiaries onto the main railroad station, they were coned by searchlights. Right away, flak began to explode around the plane, and when the pilot went into a steep dive to evade it, the port outer engine was hit. The fire extinguishers would not put out the resulting flames, so the skipper had no option but to order the crew to bail out.

What had been drilled into him during rather uninteresting parachute drill lectures was quickly recalled as Frank jumped through the escape hatch and into the dark night. Even though everything worked well, bailing out at night was not a lot of fun. Nor was hitting the frozen ground at a bone-shaking twelve miles per hour.

But nothing was broken; and then his lessons on escape came to Frank's mind. For two days, he hid in the woods by day and walked the roads by night, reading the rice-paper maps included in his escape kit, which were designed to show the way to freedom. Then he tried his luck on the train, and this was his undoing; he was attempting to ride without a ticket. He was apprehended by the train and station staff, who handed him over to the *Luftwaffe*. The balance of Frank's war was spent in *Stalag Luft* VIIIB, Lamsdorf.

Before the war, Frank had planned on becoming a pharmacist, but with what he learned during the war and in the prison camp, he decided economics was much more his line. The result was a successful career as a professor of economics at various universities. Frank is retired and living in Calgary.

There are many other Locals that I have yet to hear from, but in the absence of an escape story, I can only offer a few words of what several encountered on their fatal day. **David Rosenthal**, of obvious parentage, bailed out of a Halifax II on January 21, 1944, while bombing Magdeburg in Germany. Captured almost immediately by a rather unsmiling German unit, Dave dazzled them with his clear Irish accent.

Davie is a puzzle! A successful career in the real estate industry seems to be what he is most noted for, but his penchant for attracting lovely ladies really sets him above the crowd. Maybe it is the Irish accent!

But **Wilkie Wanless** was another case again. All I really know about his fatal day was that he was on his twenty-fourth trip over occupied Europe, and it was on my birthday. Perhaps the best way to describe Wilkie's "ordeal" is by the poem that I wrote after he said I had not fought in the same war as he did.

A Different War

A different war he said he fought,
While I was taking leave.
He landed in a German camp,
Which caused a few to grieve.

But me, I fought the honour war,
On the streets of London Town.
The Girls that Wilkie left behind,
I would never have let down.

I knew they sobbed because he left,
I knew they missed his kiss.
I thought that if I took his place,
They'd never miss the bliss.

So, when you say the war I fought,
Was not the same as yours,
Just think of all the souls I saved,
While taking furlough tours.

who packed your parachute?

In all of the stories, and for all of the successful jumps, who packed your parachute?

We all have our "parachute packer," whether it be the physical instrument made from nylon, or almost anything else we do in life. Very few of us know who the person was that ensured all Caterpillars of a safe fall to earth; I tried to find out after the war, but it seems these packers will forever remain anonymous to those of us who shall forever remain grateful.

The story from one pilot illustrates just how important the packer can be.

Charles Plumb was a jet fighter pilot over Vietnam and, after seventy-five combat missions, his plane was destroyed by a surface-to-air missile. Plumb ejected and parachuted into enemy hands. He was captured and spent six years in a Communist

Vietnamese prison. He survived the ordeal, and now lectures on lessons learned from that experience.

One day, when Plumb and his wife were sitting in a restaurant, a man at another table came up and said, "You're Plumb! You flew jet fighters in Vietnam from the aircraft carrier *Kitty Hawk*. You were shot down!"

"How in the world did you know that?" asked Plumb.

"I packed your parachute," the man replied.

Plumb gasped in surprise and gratitude. The man pumped his hand and said, "I guess it worked!" Plumb assured him, "It sure did. If your chute hadn't worked, I wouldn't be here today."

Plumb couldn't sleep that night, thinking about that man. Plumb says, "I kept wondering what he might have looked like in a navy uniform: a white hat, a bib in the back, and bell-bottom trousers. I wondered how many times I might have seen him and not even said, "Good morning," "How are you?" or anything at all; because, you see, I was a fighter pilot and he was just a sailor.

Plumb thought of the many hours the sailor had spent on a long wooden table in the bowels of the ship, carefully weaving the shrouds and folding the silks of each chute, holding in his hands each time the fate of someone he didn't even know.

Now, Plumb asks his audience, "Who's packing your parachute?"

Everyone has someone who provides what he or she needs to make it through the day. Plumb also points out that he needed many kinds of parachutes when his plane was shot down over enemy territory—he needed his physical parachute, his mental parachute, his emotional parachute, and his spiritual parachute.

He called on all these supports before reaching safety. Doesn't all this sound a little familiar to those of us who have had to rely on our parachutes to bring us safely back to earth?

Sometimes in the daily challenges that life gives us, we miss what is really important. We may fail to say hello, please, or thank you, congratulate someone on something wonderful that has happened to them, give a compliment, or just do something nice for no reason.

As we go through this week, this month, this year, recognize those people who packed your parachute.

From an e-mail letter received from Lloyd (Hap) Geddes, a Caterpillar and former P.O.W.

grapes and caterpillars

The Story of the Caterpillar Shiraz

Although the skies over Europe, Asia, Africa, and many other wine-producing regions were alive with parachutes during the war, few flyers fell where the landing would be the most enjoyed: into a winery after successfully escaping from their doomed airplanes by parachute.

But that gross mistake is about to be rectified! There is a winery that is about to reward those people who strapped on the parachute and took their lives into their hands by jumping into the unknown. Sadly, at this late date, many Caterpillars have "cast off their mortal coils" and will be unable to partake of the rewards being offered. However, I am certain those of us still left will be glad to fill the void.

Lindsay Hunting, owner of Slaley Cellars, a winemaker of South Africa, advised the author that he had such an admiration for Caterpillars that he was allocating a quantity of his Reserve Shiraz 1999 for them. As soon as a Caterpillar is located, identified, and confirmed, a Magnum of the wine will be available to that person. (Smacks of the author's earlier offer to establish a Scotch distillery in the Highlands based on the number of rip cords still outstanding: *For every rip cord not returned to the station of the Caterpillar's departure, one bottle of good Scotch is owed to the person who packed the original parachute.*)

But the generosity of Lindsay Hunting does not just appear out of the blue; it has a long background in the association of the Hunting Family with aviation. Their history predates the twentieth century, when they were shipowners and landowners residing near the village of Slaley, outside of Newcastle, England. A grandson of the founder, Gerald Lindsay Hunting, was badly wounded during World War I at Ypres, and discharged from the army. On his recovery, he joined the Royal Flying Corps, where he served until after the end of the war.

This was the start of a long family association with aircraft operating and manufacture. During World War II, deep in old quarry tunnels at Llanberis near Caemarfon in Wales, they built Lancaster fuselages, Stirling bomb doors, Wellington tail frames, bomb beams, etc. In September of 1944, the company purchased the Percival Aircraft Company. By the end of hostilities, a factory at Luton was constructing Airspeed Oxfords and De Havilland Mosquitoes, as well as their other products. They also had facilities at Tollerton in Nottingham for work on Lancasters.

At one time, the famous "Legless Ace" of the Royal Air Force, and Caterpillar, Douglas Bader, worked for the family.

In the late '80s, the Hunting Group purchased Irvin Aerospace, producers of parachutes, and so acquired their interest in Caterpillars, which had been a secret interest of Lindsay's since childhood. After reaching adulthood, he took up parachuting, but after breaking his back on his fourth jump, switched to the safer job of pilot. He received his private licence in 1985 and his commercial licence in 1989. A few years later, Lindsay took over the farming operation from his father, Martin, and started Slaley Cellars. And so began the story of the Caterpillar Shiraz.

A humorous side to the aviation connection occurred in the year 2000 when Lindsay visited Hamburg, Germany, on a promotion trip for their new winery. Unfortunately, planned interviews were cancelled because an unexploded RAF bomb had been discovered on the outskirts of town, and the media were off to cover that. Apparently, it was a ten-ton blockbuster, which could have been dropped only by a Lancaster. That was when Lindsay thought that his introduction to the German wine market quite possibly had been thwarted by their own aircraft construction efforts of the war.

Late in the century, the Hunting Group divested themselves of all their interests in defence, and so lost the Irvin connection. However, Lindsay still retains his regard for Caterpillars and, through Slaley Cellars, hopes to honour them with his Shiraz offer. He has made around 400 Magnums from his '99 vintage, which are available to Caterpillars who get in touch with him.

However, filled Magnum bottles are expensive to ship around the world, so Lindsay would prefer that each prospect visit Slaley Winery, near Stellenbosch, South Africa, to pick up the gift. Besides the obvious qualification of having saved his or her life by parachute, another requirement is that each must supply the story of that escape.

Well, nothing is totally free in this world!

Grapes and Caterpillars

тhe Dedication

I n a mixture of stories such as are contained in this book, it is sometimes difficult to choose a subject or a person to whom the dedication is made. It was not difficult in this case. During the windup of the writing and editing of all these Caterpillar tales, I (the Author) celebrated my eightieth birthday. I had planned a modest party to celebrate the day and thank my many friends for their friendship and help. The date was October 3rd, 2003.

One of the guests I had hoped would be able to attend was a lady living in France, who had been of immeasurable help to me once I had finished my "entrance exams" to the Caterpillar Club. Josette Ponchaux was the young lady who happened to live next door to where I was hiding, and who made life so very pleasant during my stay in her town.

Presently living in the town of Bourg La Reine (Queensburg)—which is part of Paris—under her married name of Mme. Josette Baudinot, she and her husband Serge were unable to attend the party. However, Josette did send me a letter with the following words (in somewhat fractured English):

> "During spring 1944, when I met John Neal in
> Aisne, which had been declared as the 'Prohibited
> Zone' under the German occupation, that is, the

BLESS YOU, *Brother Irvin*

most supervised zone, we, the French people, were waiting with great hope mixed with distress, for the Allies to come and set us free. It seemed to take shape from day to day. We followed passionately all that was happening, thanks to the BBC to which we listened clandestinely and to the Resistance of which we had the echo.

"One day my neighbour called me and told me that I should keep the whole secret to myself about what she was going to show me. I was quite intrigued. I entered into her kitchen and found myself in front of a young man who was seated and whom I had never seen before. He appeared to me a little anxious and uneasy.

"This was our conversation:

'You don't know him?' asked she.

'No.'

'Eh well, he fell from the sky.'

"Immediately, I understood. I made out what he had just lived and I felt so shattered that my eyes filled with tears.

"He represented the Freedom which was beginning to dawn and it was wonderful. I was nineteen years old then; he has been my friend since that memorable day. That is why I am proud and happy to tell you these few words in the preface of his book."

Josette Baudinot, born Ponchaux

In view of the memories associated with this friendship, I dedicate one-half of *Bless You, Brother Irvin* to my wonderful friend, Josette Baudinot, née Ponchaux.

The other half of my dedication is reserved for those eight young airmen who trained with me (out of a class of eighteen) and were never given the chance of becoming Caterpillars. I also include the young airman Victor Knox, who was serving as our tail gunner on the night we were shot down, and who was never given the chance to bail out as I did. Now they lie in different locations around Europe. At the time of this writing, we were going through what we call "Remembrance Day" (Veterans Day in the USA), and it was my thought that I should remember those who did not live to join us on this day, November 11th. They were so young!

Victor Knox - Tail Gunner
Eric Cutler - Classmate
Henri Mallette - Classmate
James McCreary - Classmate
Charles Panton - Classmate
Stuart Preston - Classmate
Ronald Smalley - Classmate
Chester Szymanski - Classmate
Harry Trueman - Classmate

As is stated during the Remembrance ceremonies:

They shall grow not old, as we who are left grow old; age shall not weary them nor the years condemn. At the going down of the sun, and in the morning, we shall remember them.

Mme. Josette Baudinot (née Ponchaux).

glossary

AIRCRAFT

B-17	Boeing four-engine bomber of the USAAF
B-24	Boeing 24, a four-engine, high-wing bomber of the USAAF
Bristol Blenheim	Twin-engine RAF bomber
FW-190	Focke Wulf 190, a German single-engine fighter
Halifax	A four-engine RAF bomber
Hurricane	A single-engine RAF fighter
JU-88	Junkers 88, a German twin-engine fighter/bomber
Lancaster	A four-engine RAF bomber
Marauder	A twin-engine USAAF medium bomber
ME-109	Messerschmitt 109, a German single-engine fighter
ME-110	Messerschmitt 110, a German twin-engine fighter
Mosquito	A twin-engine RAF fighter/bomber
Spitfire	A single-engine RAF fighter

CREW POSITIONS AND RANKS

B/A	Bomb aimer
Eng	Engineer
F/L	Flight lieutenant (captain)
F/O	Flying officer (1st lieutenant)
G/C	Group captain (colonel)
MU/G	Mid-upper gunner
Nav	Navigator
P/O	Pilot officer (2nd lieutenant)
R/G	Rear or tail gunner
Skipper	The pilot, whatever rank
S/L	Squadron leader (major)
W/C	Wing commander (lieutenant colonel)
W/OP	Wireless operator

MISCELLANEOUS

Achtung	German for "attention" (used for readers falling asleep)
AFB	Air force base
AVRO	A.V. Rowe Aircraft Company
BBC	The British Broadcasting Corporation
D-Ring or Rip Cord	The release method for parachutes
Dinghy	An inflatable boat, carried in each airplane, and in which airmen could, normally, safely depart from a sinking airplane after it lands on the water
East Grinstead	Hospital where doctors repaired the badly burned and damaged bodies of airmen
Flak	Anti-aircraft fire (or nagging)
IAF	Indian Air Force
Luftwaffe	The German air force
Mae West	Flotation device worn by all airmen to ensure they would float if downed over water. It imparted the same general characteristics as those of Miss West, at her best.
May Day	Distress call
MGB-503	One of the motorized gunboats used to bring airmen back to England
Port	Left side of ship or aircraft
POW	Anybody who finds himself landing around unfriendly people
RAAF	Royal Australian Air Force
RAF	Royal Air Force
RCAF	Royal Canadian Air Force
Reseau **Shelburne**	A line of Resistance members dedicated to saving lost airmen and returning them to England. There were also the "O'Leary Line" and the "Comet Line."
RNZAF	Royal New Zealand Air Force
Schlage Musik	Upward-pointed machine guns on *Luftwaffe* night fighters.
Sloshed	The usual slang for over-imbibing (quite often just before an operation)
Starboard	Right side of ship or aircraft
TAZI	Trailing antenna (dangerous if met while bailing out)
The Drink	Slang for the ocean, the English Channel, or anything wet that awaits a descent by parachute
U-boat	German submarine (most unfriendly to airmen who have landed nearby; see "POW")
USAAF	United States Army Air Force

about the author

Born in Verdun, Quebec, on October 3rd, 1923, John served with the Royal Canadian Air Force from 1942 to 1945. During this time, he flew as a bomb aimer with #419 "Moose" Squadron operations over Europe. Shot down over France on his thirteenth trip, John evaded capture for five months before returning to England, and home.

After the war, John completed a degree at McGill University, and then worked in the chemical industry in sales, product research and development, and consulting, until his retirement in 1988. It was then he found his true love—writing. He has penned a number of books, such as *The Lucky Pigeon*, *Rusty's Mountain*, *The Scheidhauer Experience*, and a series of humorous "Flightplan" travel stories. John also dabbles in poetry.

For many years he has been collecting stories of bailouts from around the world, and this has finally resulted in the book *Bless You, Brother Irvin*. He hopes you enjoy reading it as much as he did collecting the stories.

To order more copies of

BLESS YOU,
Brother Irvin
the caterpillar club story

by John A. Neal

Contact:

GENERAL STORE

PUBLISHING HOUSE

499 O'Brien Road, Box 415
Renfrew, Ontario Canada K7V 4A6
Telephone: 1-800-465-6072
Fax: (613) 432-7184
www.gsph.com

VISA and MASTERCARD accepted.